THE NEW ASTROLOGY

Sagittarius

BY
SUZANNE WHITE

The New Astrology

Sagittarius

A Unique Synthesis of the World's Two Greatest
Astrological Systems: Chinese and Western
By
SUZANNE WHITE

The New Astrology
Suzanne White

TABLE OF CONTENTS

What Is the *New Astrology?*

The New Astrology compares Western signs to Chinese signs and comes up with 144 *new* signs. If you are a Sagittarius and were born in 1949, then you are a Sagittarius/Ox. Simple. Take your regular, familiar astrological sign and match it with the animal sign of the year you were born. Now you have your New astrological sign.

Everybody has a dual nature. Some people are naturally greedy and grasping about money. But surprise! These same people can be generous to a fault in emotional ways, strewing sentiment and affection on their entourage like Santa Claus on a gift binge. People are complicated. They baffle us with their contradictory behavior. We even confuse ourselves with our own haunting ambivalences. How come you get along with Jack and care so much about him when in fact he gets on your nerves? Jack has an abrasive personality. You know that. But you can't help liking the guy. He fascinates you. Why? It's a dilemma. With a solution.

In order to understand your attraction for the difficult Jack, so as to comprehend the opacities of your own soul, by yourself, without the aid of a shrink or a psychiatrist, all you have to do is read *The New Astrology*, apply it to your day-to-day life, and you're off and running.

Why Does the New Astrology Work?

The New Astrology work attempts to help us understand human behavior within the universe through the "marriage" of occidental and oriental astrologies. By blending the western Sun Signs with the Chinese Animal signs, we can view many more sides of a person's character than we do with a single type of astrology.

The Chinese have divided time differently from us Westerners. Whereas we have 100-year centuries, the Chinese have periods of sixty years. We divide our centuries into ten decades. The Chinese divide their sixty-year spans into "dozencades" or twelve-year periods.

In the West, we divide our year up twelve times by its moons. Each 28- to 30-day month has its own astrological name. Every year our cycle begins anew. In the East, each year within the twelve-year dozencade has its own astrological name. At the end of each twelve-year period the Chinese cycle begins anew.

The twelve occidental months have celestial sign names: *Aries, Taurus, Gemini, Cancer, Leo, Virgo, Libra, Scorpio, Sagittarius, Capricorn, Aquarius, Pisces*. The twelve oriental years have animal sign names: *Rat, Ox, Tiger, Cat, Dragon, Snake, Horse,*

Goat, Monkey, Rooster, Dog, Pig. In both cases the astrological sign name refers to the character of people born under its influence.

So, in fact, everybody in the world has not just one but two main astrological signs. A Western "month" sign and an Oriental "year" sign. One sign is complementary to the other. Taken together, they show us more about the individual than either one can on its own. In the New Astrology, if someone is born in Aries and is also born in a Horse year, that person's New Astrology sign is *Aries/Horse*. Aries/Horses, as you will see, are not the same as Aries/Cats or Aries/Tigers.

There are 144 (12x12) New Astrology signs. Each is a combined East/West sign. The point of this exercise is to refine our understanding of human nature. Through the New Astrology we can learn to get along better with our friends, family and loved ones. We can find out why we tend not to harmonize with certain people. We can improve our knowledge of them, and of ourselves.

What is this book about?

This book is about **SAGITTARIUS**. All 12 kinds of Sagittarius. We begin with the Sagittarius/Rat and end with the Sagittarius/Pig. But before we discover all twelve types of Sagittarius, let's look closely at the Sagittarius sign's qualities and faults.

<table>
<tr><td rowspan="7">SAGITTARIUS</td></tr>
<tr><td>**Dates**</td><td>November 23 to December 21</td></tr>
<tr><td>**Ruler**</td><td>Jupiter</td></tr>
<tr><td>**Element**</td><td>Fire</td></tr>
<tr><td>**Quality**</td><td>Mutable</td></tr>
<tr><td>**Characteristics**</td><td>Cheerfulness, Valor, Open handedness, Solicitude, Honor, Reason</td></tr>
<tr><td>**Sins**</td><td>Outspokenness, Vacillation, Recklessness, Carelessness, Bad manners, Contradiction</td></tr>
</table>

The first thing I notice as I glance down my list of Sagittarians is that they all have an amazing ability to care for others. I've been to about a hundred doctors in my frail little life and about fifty of them have been Sagittarians! These people just love being helpful.

Many Sagittarians are bachelors. I know quite a number of Sagittarian subjects who never got married or else got married once and after three days ran off and never tried it again. The Sagittarian is an independent human being who seeks adventure even in the banal. Seeing the same face every day in the same surroundings doing and saying the same things is not the Sagittarian's idea of paradise. Rather, he or she could be content with a roof, a dog, plenty to eat (but nothing too exorbitantly expensive), a good position in the world and lots of dear friends around him to accept all his moral and material handouts.

Sagittarians are often planning or returning from a trip. They are drawn to travel and motion, always seeking to grow their knowledge of unusual cultures and exciting new places. Those group holidays where people tap on rocks in the Sahara or clamber over miles of rugged terrain to locate a lost shrine are loaded with curious Sagittarians.

As a result, Sagittarians prosper in jobs that permit mobility and allow them to meet new people. They function best in relationships which leave them lots of leeway to come and go as they please. They are happiest when learning and growing and are repelled by sameness and routine.

Sagittarian women are particularly success-oriented. They like to run things, *their way*, and are not usually squeamish about how many dead bodies they have lo walk over in the process.

Need some advice on a dicey sublet or a special color of typewriter ribbon made only in the Philippines? Ask a Sagittarian. They will bounce right out and find you exactly what you want. Then, proudly and with almost childlike enthusiasm, old Sag will ring you up to ask, "How many of those ochre typewriter ribbons did you want?" You ask for it. He's got it. Sagittarius notices everything, pays close attention to details and remembers everybody's birthday. If not by heart, then jotted down in a little date book specially kept for this purpose.

My Sagittarius sister-in-law, Nicole, not only remembers everybody's birthday, but she knows how many times you have bought this certain kind of perfume since last June and whether or not you are the kind of person who likes Breton oysters. It's not that Nicole's memory is so fantastic, although she's very clever. It's that she really, really cares. "Oh..." she'll say after I haven't seen her for ten months and she visits me in Paris. "You cut your hair and had it pushed back over the ears. You lost a pound and you moved the couch. I think you look terrific. How did you ever get that makeup to be so smooth?" When Sagittarius women love somebody, they are not afraid to show it

Sometimes, because they are very direct, Sagittarians tend to blurt out remarks that might have been better left unsaid. "You had your eyes done!" cried a Sagittarian friend when I met him at Orly Airport. I nearly fainted. Worse, I hadn't had my eyes done at all. He was so embarrassed, poor thing. He meant well. He meant to say, "You look terrific," the way my discreet sister-in-law has learned to. But instead, he mentioned my eyes, which 1 always think have giant bags under them and are better not discussed.

Even so, Sagittarian people have an outstanding ability to cheer one up. If I am ever sad or feeling sorry for myself, I call up my Sagittarian friends. They love to chat and will always have a funny story to tell, a nice cup of hot tea prepared for you or a bottle of your favorite rosé on ice. You can tell your Sagittarian friend anything you are feeling and he won't be shocked. The Sagittarian is the soul of comprehension and exudes good will. Find yourself one for a friend. You won't regret it.

Now to the **Chinese Calendar and Signs.** Here is a mere sampling of the character of the Chinese Animal signs you will encounter in this book. For all the information on Chinese Animal signs please get my e-book THE NEW CHINESE ASTROLOGY© at: http://www.suzannewhite.com

The Chinese Calendar (1900 to 2020)

Year	Sign	Element	Year begins	Year ends
1900	Rat	Metal	01/31/1900	02/18/1901
1901	Ox	Metal	02/19/1901	02/07/1902
1902	Tiger	Water	02/08/1902	01/28/1903
1903	Cat	Water	01/29/1903	02/15/1904
1904	Dragon	Wood	02/16/1904	02/03/1905
1905	Snake	Wood	02/04/1905	01/24/1906
1906	Horse	Fire	01/25/1906	02/12/1907
1907	Goat	Fire	02/13/1907	02/01/1908
1908	Monkey	Earth	02/02/1908	01/21/1909
1909	Rooster	Earth	01/22/1909	02/09/1910
1910	Dog	Metal	02/10/1910	01/29/1911
1911	Pig	Metal	01/30/1911	02/17/1912
1912	Rat	Water	02/18/1912	02/05/1913
1913	Ox	Water	02/06/1913	01/25/1914
1914	Tiger	Wood	01/26/1914	02/13/1915
1915	Cat	Wood	02/14/1915	02/02/1916
1916	Dragon	Fire	02/03/1916	01/22/1917
1917	Snake	Fire	01/23/1917	02/10/1918
1918	Horse	Earth	02/11/1918	01/31/1919
1919	Goat	Earth	02/01/1919	02/19/1920
1920	Monkey	Metal	02/20/1920	02/07/1921
1921	Rooster	Metal	02/08/1921	01/27/1922
1922	Dog	Water	01/28/1922	02/15/1923
1923	Pig	Water	02/16/1923	02/04/1924

1924	Rat	Wood	02/05/1924	01/23/1925
1925	Ox	Wood	01/24/1925	02/12/1926
1926	Tiger	Fire	02/13/1926	02/01/1927
1927	Cat	Fire	02/02/1927	01/22/1928
1928	Dragon	Earth	01/23/1928	02/09/1929
1929	Snake	Earth	02/10/1929	01/29/1930
1930	Horse	Metal	01/30/1930	02/16/1931
1931	Goat	Metal	02/17/1931	02/05/1932
1932	Monkey	Water	02/06/1932	01/25/1933
1933	Rooster	Water	01/26/1933	02/13/1934
1934	Dog	Wood	02/14/1934	02/03/1935
1935	Pig	Wood	02/04/1935	01/23/1936
1936	Rat	Fire	01/24/1936	02/10/1937
1937	Ox	Fire	02/11/1937	01/30/1938
1938	Tiger	Earth	01/31/1938	02/18/1939
1939	Cat	Earth	02/19/1939	02/07/1940
1940	Dragon	Metal	02/08/1940	01/26/1941
1941	Snake	Metal	01/27/1941	02/14/1942
1942	Horse	Water	02/15/1942	02/04/1943
1943	Goat	Water	02/05/1943	01/24/1944
1944	Monkey	Wood	01/25/1944	02/12/1945
1945	Rooster	Wood	02/13/1945	02/01/1946
1946	Dog	Fire	02/02/1946	01/21/1947
1947	Pig	Fire	01/22/1947	02/09/1948
1948	Rat	Earth	02/10/1948	01/28/1949
1949	Ox	Earth	01/29/1949	02/16/1950
1950	Tiger	Metal	02/17/1950	02/05/1951
1951	Cat	Metal	02/06/1951	01/26/1952

1952	Dragon	Water	01/27/1952	02/13/1953
1953	Snake	Water	02/14/1953	02/02/1954
1954	Horse	Wood	02/03/1954	01/23/1955
1955	Goat	Wood	01/24/1955	02/11/1956
1956	Monkey	Fire	02/12/1956	01/30/1957
1957	Rooster	Fire	01/31/1957	02/17/1958
1958	Dog	Earth	02/18/1958	02/07/1959
1959	Pig	Earth	02/08/1959	01/27/1960
1960	Rat	Metal	01/28/1960	02/14/1961
1961	Ox	Metal	02/15/1961	02/04/1962
1962	Tiger	Water	02/05/1962	01/24/1963
1963	Cat	Water	01/25/1963	02/12/1964
1964	Dragon	Wood	02/13/1964	02/01/1965
1965	Snake	Wood	02/02/1965	01/20/1966
1966	Horse	Fire	01/21/1966	02/08/1967
1967	Goat	Fire	02/09/1967	01/29/1968
1968	Monkey	Earth	01/30/1968	02/16/1969
1969	Rooster	Earth	02/17/1969	02/05/1970
1970	Dog	Metal	02/06/1970	01/26/1971
1971	Pig	Metal	01/27/1971	02/14/1972
1972	Rat	Water	02/15/1972	02/02/1973
1973	Ox	Water	02/03/1973	01/22/1974
1974	Tiger	Wood	01/23/1974	02/10/1975
1975	Cat	Wood	02/11/1975	01/30/1976
1976	Dragon	Fire	01/31/1976	02/17/1977
1977	Snake	Fire	02/18/1977	02/06/1978
1978	Horse	Earth	02/07/1978	01/27/1979
1979	Goat	Earth	01/28/1979	02/15/1980

1980	Monkey	Metal	02/16/1980	02/04/1981
1981	Rooster	Metal	02/05/1981	01/24/1982
1982	Dog	Water	01/25/1982	02/12/1983
1983	Pig	Water	02/13/1983	02/01/1984
1984	Rat	Wood	02/02/1984	02/19/1985
1985	Ox	Wood	02/20/1985	02/08/1986
1986	Tiger	Fire	02/09/1986	01/28/1987
1987	Cat	Fire	01/29/1987	02/16/1988
1988	Dragon	Earth	02/17/1988	02/05/1989
1989	Snake	Earth	02/06/1989	02/26/1990
1990	Horse	Metal	01/27/1990	02/14/1991
1991	Goat	Metal	02/15/1991	02/03/1992
1992	Monkey	Water	02/04/1992	01/22/1993
1993	Rooster	Water	01/23/1993	02/09/1994
1994	Dog	Wood	02/10/1994	01/30/1995
1995	Pig	Wood	01/31/1995	02/18/1996
1996	Rat	Fire	02/19/1996	02/06/1997
1997	Ox	Fire	02/07/1997	01/27/1998
1998	Tiger	Earth	01/28/1998	02/15/1999
1999	Cat	Earth	02/16/1999	02/04/2000
2000	Dragon	Metal	02/05/2000	01/23/2001
2001	Snake	Metal	01/24/2001	02/11/2002
2002	Horse	Water	02/12/2002	01/31/2003
2003	Goat	Water	02/01/2003	01/21/2004
2004	Monkey	Wood	01/22/2004	02/08/2005
2005	Rooster	Wood	02/09/2005	01/28/2006
2006	Dog	Fire	01/29/2006	02/17/2007
2007	Pig	Fire	02/18/2007	02/06/2008

2008	Rat	Earth	02/07/2008	01/25/2009
2009	Ox	Earth	01/26/2009	02/13/2010
2010	Tiger	Metal	02/14/2010	02/02/2011
2011	Cat	Metal	02/03/2011	01/22/2012
2012	Dragon	Water	01/23/2012	02/09/2013
2013	Snake	Water	02/10/2013	01/30/2014
2014	Horse	Wood	01/31/2014	02/18/2015
2015	Goat	Wood	02/19/2015	02/07/2016
2016	Monkey	Fire	02/08/2016	01/27/2017
2017	Rooster	Fire	01/28/2017	02/15/2018
2018	Dog	Earth	02/16/2018	02/04/2019
2019	Pig	Earth	02/05/2019	01/24/2020

RATS ARE:

*Seductive • Energetic • Of good counsel • Charming
Meticulous • Sociable • Jolly • Persistent • Humorous • Intellectual
Lovable • Sentimental • Generous • Honest*

BUT THEY CAN ALSO BE:

*Profiteering • Manipulative • Agitated • Gamblers
Greedy • Petty • Suspicious • Disquiet • Tiresome
Destructive • Power-hungry*

OXEN ARE:

*Patient • Hard-working • Familial • Methodical • Loners • Leaders
Proud • Equilibriated • Reserved • Precise • Confidence-inspiring • Eloquent
Self-sacrificing • Original • Silent • Long-suffering • Strong • Tenacious*

BUT THEY CAN ALSO BE:

*Slow • Loutish • Stubborn • Sore losers • Authoritarian
Conventional • Resistant to change • Misunderstood
Rigid • Vindictive • Jealous*

TIGERS ARE:

*Hugely generous • Well-mannered • Courageous •Self-assured • Leaders
Protectors • Honorable • Noble • Active • Liberal-minded • Magnetic • Lucky Strong
Authoritative Sensitive • Deep-thinking • Passionate • Venerable*

BUT THEY CAN ALSO BE:

*Undisciplined • Uncompromising • Vain • Rash
In constant danger • Disobedient • Hasty • Hotheaded
Stubborn • Disrespectful of rules • Quarrelsome*

CAT/RABBITS ARE:

Discreet • Refined • Virtuous • Social • Tactful
Unflappable • Sensitive • Companionable • Solicitous • Ambitious
Gifted • Forgiving • Prudent • Traditional • Hospitable • Clever

BUT THEY CAN ALSO BE:

Old-fashioned • Pedantic • Thin-skinned
Devious • Aloof • Private • Dilettantish • Fainthearted
Squeamish • Hypochondriacal

DRAGONS ARE:

Scrupulous • Sentimental • Enthusiastic • Intuitive • Shrewd
Tenacious • Healthy • Influential • Vital • Generous • Spirited
Captivating • Artistic • Admirable • Lucky • Successful • Autonomous

BUT THEY CAN ALSO BE:
Disquiet • Stubborn • Willful • Demanding
Irritable • Loud-mouthed • Malcontent • Other-worldly
Impetuous • Infatuate • Judgmental

SNAKES ARE:

Wise • Cultivated • Cerebral • Accommodating • Intuitive
Attractive • Amusing • Lucky • Sympathetic • Elegant • Soft-spoken
Well-bred • Compassionate • Philosophical • Calm • Decisive

BUT THEY CAN ALSO BE:

Ostentatious • Sore losers • Tight-fisted
Extravagant • Presumptuous • Possessive • Vengeful
Self-critical • Phlegmatic • Lazy • Fickle

HORSES ARE:

Amiable • Eloquent • Skillful • Self-possessed
Quick-witted • Athletic • Entertaining • Charming • Independent
Powerful • Hard-working • Jolly • Sentimental • Frank • Sensual

BUT THEY CAN ALSO BE:

Selfish • Weak • Hotheaded • Ruthless
Rebellious • Pragmatic • Foppish • Tactless
Impatient • Unfeeling • Predatory

GOATS ARE:

Elegant • Creative • Intelligent • Well-mannered • Sweet-natured
Tasteful • Inventive • Homespun • Persevering • Lovable • Delicate
Artistic • Amorous • Malleable • Altruistic • Peace-loving

BUT THEY CAN ALSO BE:

Pessimistic • Fussbudgets • Dissatisfied
Capricious • Intrusive • Undisciplined • Dependent
Irresponsible • Unpunctual • Insecure

MONKEYS ARE:

Acutely intelligent • Witty • Inventive • Affable • Problem-solvers
Independent • Skillful business people • Achievers • Enthusiastic
Lucid • Nimble • Passionate • Youthful • Fascinating • Clever

BUT THEY CAN ALSO BE:

Tricky tacticians • Vain • Dissimulators
Opportunistic • Long-winded • Not all that trustworthy
Unfaithful • Adolescent • Unscrupulous

ROOSTERS ARE:

Frank • Vivacious • Courageous • Resourceful • Attractive
Talented • Generous • Sincere • Enthusiastic • Conservative • Industrious
Stylish • Amusing • Contemplative • Popular • Adventurous • Self-assured

BUT THEY CAN ALSO BE:

Nit-pickers • Braggarts • Quixotic
Mistrusful • Acerb • Short-sighted • Didactic
Pompous • Pedantic • Spendthrift • Brazen

DOGS ARE:

Magnanimous • Courageous • Noble • Loyal • Devoted
Attentive • Selfless • Faithful • Modest • Altruistic • Prosperous
Philosophical • Respectable • Discreet • Dutiful • Lucid • Intelligent

BUT THEY CAN ALSO BE:

Disquiet • Guarded • Introverted
Defensive • Critical • Pessimistic • F1orbidding
Cynical • Stubborn • Moralizing

PIGS ARE:

Obliging • Loyal • Scrupulous • Indulgent • Truthful
Impartial • Intelligent • Sincere • Sociable • Thorough • Cultured
Sensual • Decisive • Peaceable • Loving • Profound • Sensitive

BUT THEY CAN ALSO BE:

Naive • Defenseless • Insecure • Sardonic • Epicurean
Noncompetitive • Willful • Gullible • Earthy • Easy prey

The New Astrology

SAGITTARIUS

CHEERFULNESS	OUTSPOKENNESS
OPENHANDEDNESS	RECKLESSNESS
SOLICITUDE	BAD MANNERS
VALOR	VACILLATION
HONOR	CARELESSNESS
REASON	CONTRADICTION

"I see"

Fire, Jupiter, Mutable

RAT

INTUITION	DISSIMULATION
ATTRACTIVENESS	EXTRAVAGANCE
DISCRETION	LAZINESS
SAGACITY	CUPIDITY
CLAIRVOYANCE	PRESUMPTION
COMPASSION	EXCLUSIVITY

"I sense"

Negative Fire, Yang

The marriage of Sagittarius to Rat brings us a healthy and vivacious person full of energy and abustle with activity. The Sagittarius born Rat just about never sits still. This person likes groups and is always surrounded by guests, friends and family alike. Less charm-conscious than many Rat subjects, the Sagittarian is impatient to achieve but is not concerned about what others think of him. He or she presents a candid self-image without frills or pretense. If you like that sort of thing, you will enjoy this dynamic Sagittarian's company. If you are not attracted by his or her simplicity and directness, then you don't have to come around. It's all the same to Sagittarius/Rat. He has no time to please dissenters.

Despite being a super host or hostess and the best group animator in any crowd, this person is oddly impenetrable and reserved. The Sagittarius/Rat is not the life of the party, laugh-a-minute type. Rather, the Rat born in Sagittarius transcends the show-offy, stand-up comedian type of party thrower. This person draws people together not out of a need to be surrounded but out of a desire to see others happy, to watch them amuse themselves and to observe their interactions. The Sagittarius/Rat is the first to run to get the wine and to offer you the best chair in the house. Be comfortable. Enjoy.

In the same concerned way, the Sagittarius/Rat is a protector of loved ones. This person has the natural on-top-of-the-world quality necessary to boost the morale of ten disquieted Dogs or nervous Nellies. Not that Sagittarius/Rats spend hours stroking their pals and family members, but there is something reassuring about the presence of this guiding-light creature. One always has the feeling the Sagittarius/Rat won't forget to turn out the lights before going to bed and will be sure to lock the gate.

The people born under the dual signs of Sagittarius and Rat are opportunistic for themselves and for their loved ones. They are quick to see the worth of a situation or the use of a new person or thing. In an emergency, they act rapidly and intelligently, keeping a cool head despite their feverish action. They know how to take apart a problem and put it back together so it works. They leap at the occasion to take advantage of a stroke of luck.

Sagittarian Rats are gamblers with life. They barrel ahead when they feel the time is ripe, and they very often reap huge benefits because they have followed their nose. If you are ever in doubt about a new acquaintance's honesty or mettle, ask a Sagittarius/Rat to have a look. They know how to pick a winner.

This person is an inveterate traveler. He or she may leave home at a young age to wander, to seek a new place to settle, to find his or her own level upon which to be free to move unhampered by social convention or fusty family ties. The Sagittarian Rat has an incisive mind and is talented for rendering the human comedy in artistic ways. Such people will have the wherewithall to become leaders in charitable causes, as they feel deeply for those less fortunate than themselves. Sagittarius/Rats can make lots of money, but they are not good managers of wealth. They tend to be spendthrift and overly generous in the wrong places.

Love

In love situations this person is idealistic. Sagittarian Rats are easily disappointed in romance and may never marry. Because of their basic mistrust of all of society's demands, these people tend to shy from shoes-under-the- bed security and snug-as-a-bug-in-a-rug cliché relationships. They are fascinated by the exotic and so invested with adventure and wanderlust as to be difficult to match with a suitable life partner.

Should your affections lean to the Sagittarius/Rat and you have fallen under his or her inimitable spell, I advise you to buy a couple of seats on an airplane to Hong Kong or the Seychelles and invite your sweet Sagittarian Rat along for the ride. You may never unstick him or her from the palm trees and rickshaw lifestyle. But then you can always set up shop in a foreign land so as to be closer to your freewheeling Sagittarius/Rat and his/her projects. Don't settle in too deeply, though this person likes to keep moving. Who knows? Maybe next year you'll be moving to the Costa del Sol.

Compatibilities

Reciprocity with Aries, Leo, Libra and Aquarius/Dragons is easy for you. You can form close ties with them and you approve of their snappy approach. Leo, Libra and Aquarius/Monkeys and Oxen suit you just fine. You are wildly attracted by Libra/Goats. Tensions will arise between you and Gemini, Virgo and Pisces/Horses and Cats.

Home and Family

The Rat born in Sagittarius lives in authentic luxury. He or she will be big on paintings by the latest artists and sculpted furniture from Italy or Sweden. The Sagittarius/Rat never sacrifices comfort for luxury, however. His or her aim will always be to provide and protect family and create an ambience where huge receptions feel natural and right. Sagittarius/Rats don't mind having help in their palaces, either. They will be as nice to the service personnel as they are to their own family. This person is naturally not a snob.

With children, as with anyone who needs their help or attention, Sagittarian Rats are cleverly care-conscious. They never hover or fret over their kids. But these kind, outspoken parents never let their kids out of their minds for a minute. They are gentle and loving but they are also firm. A kid whose parent is a Sagittarius/Rat will never forget to say "Hello" to company and stand up when adults enter the room.

The Sagittarius/Rat child is likely to spread his toys and influence around a good bit even before he's out of diapers. This little tyke cannot stand to be confined, and will learn early to climb out of playpens and over high railings. The travel bug sets in early with these curious and active souls. Field trips and vacations to untrodden lands will occupy these youngsters till they are old enough to fly alone. Watch out for signs of rebellion in early adolescence. This child cannot exist in hypocritical surroundings. If there is too much unspoken tension around the home, this kid may try to pack his teddy bears and leave at age seven. Cards on the table time.

Profession

Attributes such as those of the Sagittarius/Rat are rare. This person's ability to zero in on human situations and make truth out of a single notion or vision is not common. He or she will be best utilized and happiest in peripatetic fields involving decision-making. Sagittarius/Rats are both perseverant and brave. Adventurous jobs appeal to their need for freedom.

The Sagittarius/Rat boss doesn't want power over others unless he gets truth with it. If accused of wielding blind authority, this person will find the situation intolerable. Although usually not hotheaded, Sagittarius/Rat is capable of summarily firing an employee for groveling and sniveling. He wants contact. Not obeisance.

This person is not a contented employee. He or she is always trying to get to the boss stage. They will be efficient and dutiful but never stay underlings for long. As independents these subjects work admirably well toward success.

Some professions that might please the Sagittarius/Rat are: journalist, ski instructor, sociologist, newscaster, social worker, ambulance driver, volcano explorer, geologist, sportswriter, personnel manager, lawyer, veterinarian.

Famous Sagittarius/Rats: Toulouse-Lautrec, Eugene Ionesco, Carlo Ponti, Tip O'Neill, Abbie Hoffman, Lou Rawls, Abbie Hoffmann, Amy Grant, Cathy Moriarty, Daryl Hannah, Franklin Pierece, John F. Kennedy Jr, Julianne Moore, Kenneth Branagh, Michel Tournier, Thierry Mugler, Willis Carrier.

SAGITTARIUS		OX	

CHEERFULNESS	OUTSPOKENNESS	STUBBORNNESS	INTEGRITY
OPENHANDEDNESS	RECKLESSNESS	STRENGTH OF PURPOSE	BIGOTRY
SOLICITUDE	BAD MANNERS	ELOQUENCE	PLODDING
VALOR	VACILLATION	STANDOFFISHNESS	DILIGENCE
HONOR	CARELESSNESS	INNOVATION	BIAS
REASON	CONTRADICTION	VINDICTIVENESS	STABILITY

"I see"

Fire, Jupiter, Mutable

"I sense"

Negative Water, Yin

Oxen can really accomplish a lot in life. But Sagittarius/Oxen can do more. These folks are dynamos. They are both fiery and placid. They are eloquent beyond belief. They are direct, humanistic, open-handed and strong. What's more, Sagittarians born in Ox years are ambitious for power, influence, control and prestige. They don't despise money, either.

Foresight and reason blend here, making the Sagittarius/Ox a different kind of Ox from other, more deliberate or belligerent types. This Ox is born with flair, chutzpah, style, pizzazz, charm and appeal. What they go after in life, they get. To them, success is simplicity itself. They cannot imagine failure, don't know what color it is and wouldn't recognize it if it rushed up and brained them. For the Sagittarian Ox, life is achievement. You start out small and you work hard and you get where you have always wanted to be. Any questions?

"Well, dear Sag/Ox, I do wonder why you manage to 'make it' so frequently while others of us lag behind, bring up the rear and/or positively flunk? How is it your roster of famous brave men and good women looks longer than everybody else's?" asks the Good Fairy. "Everything is relative," answers the Sagittarius/Ox. It's true. Sagittarians born in Ox years are irretrievably stolid, stuck-up and standoffish. They are impeccably idealistic and invincibly brash. They are not afraid of anything or anyone. They charge at life like an army of foot soldiers on a steady diet of Wheaties and Vitamin B12. But they are not race-around speedy. Sagittarius/Oxen are merely serious practitioners of the science of self-promotion and narrow-minded, unswerving belief in the strong-arm method of winning.

Fiery and steadfast, courageous and reckless, the Sagittarius/Ox can lead anything from a Dixieland band to an empire with good cheer and nose-in-the-air aplomb. Hitler was not a Sagittarian. Hitler wanted to kill a lot. Sagittarians like to do good in the world, help others and improve mankind. They eschew murder. And they are not shy of pain. Sagittarius/Oxen are danger-loving and will take outrageous chances to get where they care to go. They risk life and limb without blinking an eyelid for the sake of their cause or their "ism." They are not solely self-interested, though, and I have to hand it to this brand of Sagittarian—they sacrifice much comfort and security to advance their causes. Sagittarius/Oxen all have different notions of what the betterment of humanity means. But they all go after it equally hungrily. Sagittarian Oxen can have very roughshod ways and don't hesitate to air unpopular grassroots opinions. Or else they exhibit similarly uncharming conservatism. Either way, the goal is the same: Get there no matter how many little guys you have to intimidate to do so.

No. The Sagittarian Ox doesn't walk over dead bodies to get where he wants to be. He works people till they drop from exhaustion. Then he covers them sweetly with a bonny blue blanket and moves on.

Love

The Sagittarius/Ox is usually married. Or perhaps I should say he or she is unusually married. These folks often exhibit fervent fidelity in love relationships. I mean they advertise their love for their mate. They tell you how wonderful old Marsha is and what a terrific doctor Sam has learned to be and how Jim is going to save the world. It can be very flattering for both the Sagittarian Ox and the husband or wife. Otherwise

I am not sure the Sagittarius/Ox would do it. These tough customers are just a wee bit on the public side—not show-offy unless they have something to say, but they always have plenty to say.

If you love a Sagittarius/Ox and he or she doesn't return your love, you will be fiercely unhappy. This person would be very hard to lose. But should you still have a chance to nab this ultragood catch, before wedlock sets in I advise you to make it your business to understand working on a team of which you are decidedly not the coach. Learn how to track Ox footprints through the desert in the summer. You'll be needing all the breadcrumbs you can stash.

Compatibilities

Your favorite people live among the Leo, Libra and Aquarius/Rat and Snake people. A bond of communication exists between you and Aquarius/ Roosters as well. Don't try to interdepend with Dragons. You have the most difficulty with Gemini, Leo, Virgo and Pisces types. Gemini and Virgo/ Monkeys exasperate you. So do Gemini/Horses, Gemini and Virgo/Goats, and Pisces/Tigers.

Home and Family

Like everything else in their busy lives, the Sagittarian Ox's home is a showplace of efficiency, good cheer and personality. No matter who lives there, the house (or houses) is definitely a statement of the Sagittarius/Ox's preferences, tastes and attitudes. If she likes sailing, the living room will have portholes instead of windows. If he's into archery, duck!

Parenting comes naturally to this leader type. Sagittarius/Ox does everything effectively, so why not raise a couple of children, too? Why not indeed? This person should be understanding and compassionate, but he or she may be intransigent with kids and impatient with shilly-shalliers. He will surely be sincere and dutiful. Also, Sagittarius/Oxen tell a mean story. Kids like stories.

You won't believe how tremendous this child's ambition is. He or she will probably do well in school (unless somebody higher up tries to thwart him or her), shine on committees and run the baked goods sales and the fundraisers. At home, this child may be very inward and spend much time reading. He or she will definitely be sports-minded. Competition delights the Sagittarius/ Ox —even if he's only competing against himself.

Profession

This character is hell-bent to get somewhere in his or her professional life. Although business is not of primary concern to this struggler, he or she will probably make skillions. This nature is so all-encompassing and "into" life and projects and adventures and details that he cannot let even one insignificant bank statement error past him without straightening it out. They are avid for security, but that's not the point. The real moral thrust of Sagittarius/ Ox is the "shepherd" complex. They take care of everything and everybody, needed or not. And Sagittarius/Ox gets to keep half.

Boss. Definitely power post. The will to dominate is king in the makeup of the Sagittarius/Ox. Naturally, nobody will come close to this person's excellence in group situations, so if they don't get elected or chosen for the job of director, they'll simply take it. Being employed as subaltern doesn't even graze the subconscious of this hearty monster. Working alone, he or she will have factory force.

Jobs that suit the Sagittarius/Ox are: star, best-selling author, race car driver, famous anything, cartoonist, scientist, historian, president, pope, king, queen, emperor, head nurse, Mother Superior, prefect of discipline, God, pilot.

Famous people born in Sagittarius/Ox: Walt Disney, William Blake, William Buckley, Willy Brandt, Alexander Godunov, Gary Hart, Sammy Davis, Jr, Margaret Meade, Jane Fonda, Jean Marais, Alain Chapel, Jacques Dessange, Jean Mermoz, Jean Sibelius, Monica Seles, Nick Beggs.

SAGITTARIUS

TIGER

CHEERFULNESS	OUTSPOKENNESS	FERVOR	IMPETUOSITY
OPENHANDEDNESS	RECKLESSNESS	BRAVERY	HOTHEADEDNESS
SOLICITUDE	BAD MANNERS	MAGNETISM	DISOBEDIENCE
VALOR	VACILLATION	GOOD LUCK	SWAGGER
HONOR	CARELESSNESS	BENEVOLENCE	INTEMPERANCY
REASON	CONTRADICTION	AUTHORITY	ITINERANCY

"I see"

Fire, Jupiter, Mutable

"I watch"

Positive Wood, Yang

The Sagittarius born Tiger is a person who stubbornly, but charmingly, wishes to remain a child. These people love all the trappings of adventure and gadgets, space races and long journeys to faraway lands. Of course, children cannot realize such dramatic dreams. They only imagine what it's like to ride in a space ship or dive thousands of feet into the ocean's depths. Well, Sagittarius/Tigers are exactly the same. They fantasize about great adventures. But they never go further than their own backyards. Oh, yes, they will take long walks into the mountains, discover ruins and memorize each stone. But these very dear, funny people never leave home for long.

Not that Sagittarius/Tigers don't move around a lot. They most certainly do. They're the drive-overnight-to-Jerry's-and-hurry- back-twelve-hours-of-winding-roads-to-be-on-time-to-open-the-store-at-eight-in-the-morning type. Or they can take trips for business purposes and not ever feel homesick. Sagittarius/Tigers are not sticky barnacles. But they favor the path of least resistance. They'd rather stay with those of whom they are sure than go hunting up new friends or trying to seduce an unfamiliar partner. Even though adventure remains the biggest part of the Sagittarius/Tiger's life, it almost always remains inside his mind.

Socially the Sagittarius/Tiger is by turns extroverted and withdrawn. This unevenness comes, I believe, from the fact that frequently this person is forced out of his environment by his impetuous Tiger side, yet when he gets to the party, he's instantly bored and wishes he were home inside his head again. Tiger keeps trying to erupt this person onto the social scene but Sagittarius is more interested in keeping him occupied with books and causes. It happens that the Sagittarius/Tiger grows so uncomfortable with the pressures of interaction in society—especially with unfamiliar people—that, out of embarrassment, he misbehaves. The Sagittarius/Tiger can be that woman in the center of the room with the big mouth, telling off-color jokes and secretly wishing she were anywhere but there.

This person is a keen observer. He or she may attend gatherings or join in group activities solely for the purpose of watching. Sagittarius/Tiger is aware of everything, sensitive to a forearm hair to tone and atmosphere. He or she will be fascinated by novelty and eccentricity. If the Sagittarius/Tiger becomes interested in something, he or she will usually track it down and find out all there is to know about it. In this way the Sagittarius/Tiger builds an inner library of characters about whom he knows everything. It's a singular hobby, but one native to the Sagittarius/Tiger. I call it "people-collecting."

Of course this person is dealt a reckless and outspoken personality by birth. He is a victim of both Sagittarian and Tiger recklessness and swagger hotheadedness and vacillation. This makes him sometimes seem interfering when he's only trying to be helpful. But these character traits also give punch to whatever the Sagittarius/Tiger does in his life. As with other Tiger subjects, the inner goal must begin with temperance. Slow down, Sagittarius/Tiger, and think before you leap, turn your tongue around seven times before speaking and don't be so sure that public opinion is all wet. Every time you venture out into the world, try to remember to pick up a quart or two of wisdom.

Love

The romantic sector is a difficult one for the Sagittarius/Tiger. First of all, he or she will not trust easily. Tigers are always watching for flaws and picking up subtle little negative signs from others. Tigers are magnetic. Sagittarians are open-handed and solicitous. This person will seem amenable to starting a relationship. But don't get her wrong. What you can see is only the very tippy-top of a very complex iceberg. The Sagittarius/Tiger's easy generosity can quickly turn sour. She may grow cynical if disappointed. This person wants to be handled with utmost care. "Don't take me for granted!" should be inscribed on all her T-shirts. Sagittarius/Tiger is a false grandee. But then, this bumptious, kindly sort never wears her heart on her sleeve.

Should you be attracted to one of these people, step carefully. Manipulate deftly, and proceed with caution. The Sagittarian Tiger needs reassurance and loving care, but he or she will never come right out and ask for it. If I were you, I would offer this light-of-your-life type a good logical excuse for coming around to your place: Ask her if she can teach you to cook, or get him to come over and show you how to parallel park.

Compatibilities

You can depend on the love of Aries, Leo, Libra and Aquarius/Horses. They serve your causes well, and give good sound advice. Leo, Libra and Aquarius/Dogs warm your cockles as well. You can relate to their devotion. No cigar with Virgos, Geminis or Pisces born in Ox, Cat or Snake years. Virgo and Pisces/Monkeys rub you the wrong way. And Geminis born in Goat years strike you as irretrievably frivolous.

Home and Family

The Sagittarius/Tiger's home doesn't matter much to him. He would surely like it comfortable and easy to live in. But as this person is often a bachelor until middle years and doesn't really want to grow up, he or she may not bother with interior decoration. There will always be cold drinks in the fridge and a good stereo system playing fine music. But the most a Sagittarian Tiger needs is a nest for dreaming of desert islands where the nests are made of straw and the sun never sets.

This person is not overly family-oriented. Everybody can have children, however, so if he or she becomes a parent I'd reckon they would be the kind to be pals with their kids, taking them to baseball games and teaching them how to water ski. The Sagittarius/Tiger is a bit of a worrywart about others and will always take time to listen to children's woes, comfort them when they're sad and truly empathize when they are feeling misunderstood. The Sagittarian Tiger parent won't be a disciplinarian. He thinks everybody—especially he—should be free.

The Sagittarius/Tiger child will be warm and loving company for parents. He will enjoy homely pleasures like playing Monopoly with Mom and Dad, or the joys of preparing for Christmas together. The best thing about this child is his willingness to watch out for danger and to look after himself and other kids. This child will be inventive and hardworking. He or she will love electronic games.

Profession

This native is both hard-driving and tireless when at work. Sagittarius/ Tigers are ambitious people who don't much care for what others think of the means they employ to achieve their ends. For this last reason, these folks are especially able to take over on unproven projects that observers may not approve of. Sagittarian Tigers often undertake ventures of vast scope. Breadth of field appeals to their dauntless explorer side. They like to envision grandeur and pomp but don't much care for chains of command or hierarchic hypocrisies.

The Sagittarius/Tiger is not usually concerned about who's boss. He or she is most interested in getting on with work on a scale unconnected to routine. Their hope is always to escape the humdrum and somehow transcend worka-day jobs.

Although they can be efficient employees, Sagittarius/Tigers may feel they know better than their boss. These natives are best off on their own, doing their own things, running businesses or writing poems. They are good at jobs requiring frequent travel. No matter what career this fiery subject chooses, you can be sure that his life itself, morning till night, is a trip. Work is his or her best form of expression.

Jobs that might suit this person are: physicist, city planner, postman, roadie, preacher, actor/actress, athlete, journalist, fund-raiser, traveling salesperson, NASA engineer.

Some famous people born in Sagittarius/Tiger: Beethoven, Emily Dickinson, Cristina Onassis, Tracy Austin, Ed Harris, Leonard Maltin, Liane Foly, Liv Ullmann, Martin Van Buren, Sammy Davis, Tracy Austin, Wassily Kandinsky.

SAGITTARIUS		CAT / RABBIT	

CHEERFULNESS	OUTSPOKENNESS	TACT	SECRETIVENESS
OPENHANDEDNESS	RECKLESSNESS	FINESSE	SQUEAMISHNESS
SOLICITUDE	BAD MANNERS	VIRTUE	PEDANTRY
VALOR	VACILLATION	PRUDENCE	DILETTANTISM
HONOR	CARELESSNESS	LONGEVITY	HYPOCHONDRIA
REASON	CONTRADICTION	AMBITION	COMPLEXITY

"I see"

Fire, Jupiter, Mutable

"I retreat"

Negative Wood, Yin

The prudent Cat side of this couple tugs at the Sagittarian's carefree arrow till he snaps it loose. It falls to the ground before leaving the bow. In other words, in this person the recklessness of Sagittarius is defused by the Cat's virtue and sense of measure. This Sagittarian is not so brash as his brothers and sisters. A Sagittarian born in a Cat year will be sensitive to his real surroundings, aware of the need for diplomacy and, because of the Cat's serious ambition, sagaciously yoked to his or her career.

There is a spirited melancholy in this person's makeup. The Sagittarian born Cat seems to have been improved or pepped up through sorrow, tempered by loss or hurt. He is buoyant yet resigned to certain bitter truths that others prefer to ignore. The Sagittarius/Cat does not surrender to this mournful air, but rather exploits it well, using a sad smile to appeal to millions. This Sagittarian, honed to a fine edge by his careful Cat side, is able to synthesize his energies sufficiently to create a powerful self-image. Armed with this overwhelming sense of self, the Sagittarian Cat can confront almost any form of opposition. Not that he goes looking for trouble, but he is not afraid of adversity. Defiance is his natural habitat. He is bold and dares to achieve dominance and to overcome competition.

The Sagittarius/Cat is also clever enough to know how to hold on to his hard-earned position. He feeds his public just what they need to continue to be addicted to his wares. The Sagittarius/Cat dispenses great gobs of under-stated love to his fans and, as a result, he keeps them on his side. People believe in the Sagittarius/Cat because he understands the delicate blend of so-licitude and command necessary to seduce throngs.

Taking oneself seriously can be a giant pain in the neck for intimates and onlookers. But in the case of such directed people as Sagittarius/Cats, arro-gance and an air of self-satisfaction seem natural. Or at least this character knows how to make them seem natural. It's true that the Sagittarian born Cat puts himself on a pedestal and renders his person untouchable. But that's all part of the mystique that works so well. The Sagittarius/Cat is highly indivi-dualistic. His or her methods are always unusual. They may be unscrupulous, and if they don't succeed (and many don't) in enticing their audience, in captivating crowds and convincing millions, Sagittarius/Cats are wise enough to know when they are beaten.

Generally, the Sagittarius/Cat is an amiable fellow. Good cheer emanates from his aura. The Cat's sense of elegance and presentation quells almost all the Sagittarian's natural bumptiousness, and leaves us just that smidgen of vulgarity we like to call "the common touch." Cats born in Sagittarius con-form to social norms and care deeply about what others think of them. They are not easy to figure out and have no intention of becoming so. This is a brave Cat and a toned-down Sagittarian. It's a very strong marriage held toge-ther by a bond of self-interest.

Love

This person tends to engage in multiple subsequent relationships. There is a great deal of sexual energy here. Much of the energy is, of course, covert and pent up. One doesn't think of any Cat subject as a sex maniac. But the Sagit-tarius/Cat is a bit of a tom. He skulks about marking territories and claiming some that don't even belong to him. By the same token, she may not hesitate to "cat around" with other people's mates. The Sagittarius/Cat is not really unfaithful. But the need to be admired is so enormous here that sexual fidelity is impossible. Personal fidelity is, however, very serious for this character. He may love 'em and leave 'em, but he never forgets those he has cared for, and is careful to keep old friendships alive.

So you are in love with a Sagittarius/Cat? My suggestion is that you look up to him or her. Stroke and cuddle this mettlesome Cat, but don't try to keep her by the fireside. You must remember that your admiration is pleasant to her, but it's never going to be enough. This person needs to be loved by a cast of thousands. If you can keep from being jealous of your Sagittarian Cat's large following and put up with her constant primping and preening in front of prospective admirers, I guess you can take the heat. But I don't think long-term affairs or marriages with this crowd-pleaser are meant to be shared by any but self-sacrificing types.

Compatibilities

Aries, Leo and Aquarius/Dogs know instinctively how to touch your deepest emotions and make wonderful lovers for your personality type. Leo, Libra and Aquarius/Pigs are also on sympathetic terms with you, as are Aries and Aquarius/Goats. The Aries/Snake woos you without half trying. But Gemini, Virgo and Pisces/Roosters and their Tiger counterparts conspire to put you on edge. Tell them to pick on somebody their own size.

Home and Family

The Sagittarian Cat's home will be in many places at once. This nature is itinerant, and for the enormous objectives of the Sagittarius/Cat to be fulfilled, he or she must be able to travel—first class all the way. No question about that. Because he is, after all, a Cat, this person may well have one place he considers home. It will most likely be situated in the deep, remote countryside. There, he or she will have installed many comforts, a few domestics or even a second family—and of course, I almost forgot, the bodyguards.

The Sagittarius/Cat parent is very self-involved. These people often marry and have kids but they will probably leave the rearing of children to a homebody mate. This person won't be available to small fry. But as the children grow and become really able to communicate, the Sagittarius/Cat parent is likely to take a friendly interest. This parent is of the do-what-I-say-and-not-what-I-do school of education. Strict and even, boarding-school oriented.

The Sagittarius/Cat child is certainly talented for theater or music, athletics or even public speaking and debate. The ability to captivate audiences is what shows through first with this smiling babe. He or she must be encouraged to pursue these talents and given every opportunity to use them in a disciplined fashion. Try, while your Sagittarius/Cat child is still malleable and young, to increase his or her willingness to communicate on a one-to-one level. You may find this child introverted except when called upon to perform. He or she will aspire to greatness and have much appeal.

Profession

The talents of the Sagittarius/Cat, be they artistic or commercial, mechanical or technical, are all-encompassing. In other words, this person will have a major gift and be able to exploit that main talent. He or she must be very careful not to disperse energies in personal dramas or dilute talents by trying to do a variety of unrelated things. They can and will go far if they keep their sights fixed on success in one well defined area—theirs.

The Sagittarian Cat is a loner. He or she can open a business, or run a factory and manage almost any amount of work. Too, these people have a special appeal for groups. They can take charge in an office situation. But they must be allowed free rein, and as that is not always possible, I suggest this person try to be self-employed. Sagittarians born in Cat years want their own way too much to knuckle under to systems and strict hours. They are self-directed.

Some suitable careers for Sagittarius/Cats might be: politician, jockey, tour guide, diplomat, actor/actress, dancer, singer, restaurant owner, supermarket manager, religious leader, musician.

Some famous Sagittarius/Cats: Edith Piaf, Augusto Pinochet, Frank Sinatra, Aaron Carter, Brad Pitt, Milla Jovovich, Morgan Brittany, Tina Turner.

SAGITTARIUS

CHEERFULNESS	OUTSPOKENNESS
OPENHANDEDNESS	RECKLESSNESS
SOLICITUDE	BAD MANNERS
VALOR	VACILLATION
HONOR	CARELESSNESS
REASON	CONTRADICTION

"I see"

Fire, Jupiter, Mutable

DRAGON

STRENGTH	RIGIDITY
SUCCESS	MISTRUST
GOOD HEALTH	DISSATISFACTION
ENTHUSIASM	INFATUATION
PLUCK	BRAGGADOCIO
SENTIMENTALITY	VOLUBILITY

"I preside"

Positive Wood, Yang

An admirable but not always gentle character, the Sagittarius/Dragon is a warrior on the grand scale. These people are attractive and ambitious. They believe in success and forge ahead with bravura toward that aim. Never bullish or hotheaded, this character's style is gentlemanly and dignified. Sagittarius/Dragons are not afraid of danger. They take great risks and even court peril. They dance around the flame of adventure and derring-do but they rarely get seriously burned. Dragons born in Sagittarius outwit their enemies, hoist them on their own petards and invite them to lunch the next day. Victory, after all, calls for a celebration.

There is no arrogance in this method. The Sagittarius/Dragon sees no reason to snub people or lord his superiority over them. On the contrary, this character will be the jolly sort of idealist who beckons one and all to follow his dreams, brandish his flags and fly his colors. Sagittarius/Dragons are not selfish or stingy. They want the best for everybody involved—yet they definitely feel that everybody should be involved in the Sagittarian Dragon's project.

This person is a visionary and can initiate enterprises single-handedly. He or she can carry off deals and draw conclusions and make decisions without raising an eyebrow. But they don't like complication. They deplore deceit. Woe unto him who cheats a Sagittarian Dragon. The Dragon won't harm the offender. Not on your life. She will simply never trust him again, which, coming from this honorable character, is a low blow.

You see, the Sagittarius/Dragon is an optimist. He or she wants to believe in the basic goodness of mankind. These people are not naive, nor are they innocents who need protection. Rather, Sagittarius/Dragons are natural leaders who need good lieutenants, whips, exchequers, advisers, cabinet ministers, wives, husbands and careful, deliberate and faithful helpers who protect this hasty idealist from himself.

Sagittarius is outspoken and open-handed. Dragons are also very generous and giving. They both love parties and want to make life more festive. The Sagittarian and the Dragon both want to increase the scope of their operations, to encompass larger and larger groups and spheres of influence where they can impose their theories and try their methods. If left completely to their own devices, these benevolent despots might glad-hand themselves out of the race. So they must seek wise counsel and follow the advice of more conservative souls.

The combination of Sagittarius and Dragon must struggle against a little voice inside them which urges them onward no matter what. This person wants more than anything to prove that he or she can. Usually, there is no doubt in anybody's mind but that of the Sagittarian Dragon himself. Nonetheless, this person can be overly optimistic and enterprising because he wants to show the world how right he is. And very often he is right. But once in a while the Sagittarian Dragon has to pick himself up and straighten out his disjointed nose because of hasty decision-making or acting on false hunches.

The Dragon born in Sagittarius can be snappish and sometimes caustic, but is most often merciful and kind toward others. His is not a cozy fire but rather a crackling, vigorous conflagration that burns as a beacon for people he likes and wants to help. There is something of the Dragon Prince here, something noble and mythical that bespeaks munificence and power. A mightier combination one can hardly hope to find.

Love

The Dragon born in the sign of Sagittarius will marry when the time is right. Of course these people, with their hearty enthusiasms and eager aspirations, are appealing. Yet, the Sagittarius/Dragon himself is not interested solely in attraction. He will go looking for a true helpmate when he sets out in adult life. No Dragon—especially a Sagittarian Dragon—ever thinks small. This one imagines a giant future with scads of children and horses and businesses and expanded families. This Dragon is not about to marry Mickey

Mouse. This Dragon wants quality. And don't you know, he or she usually gets just that.

If one of these swashbucklers has caught your eye, I daresay you are in for quite a ride. The Sagittarius/Dragon mate will keep you on your toes, busy, busy, busy. If you are in the least phlegmatic, stay away from this vivacious dynamo. But if you want to work side by side with someone whose ideals appeal to you and whose cause you are not afraid to champion, then go after your Sagittarius/Dragon love. But don't ever disappoint this character or fail to keep your part of the bargain. Sagittarius/Dragon is a grand sentimentalist. There is nothing more cutting than the indifference of such a valorous soul.

Compatibilities

You are a very popular partner indeed. Aries, Leo, Libra and Aquarius are your compatible western astrological signs. From within their ranks you can best be loved by Aries/Ox, Tiger, Monkey and Pig; Leo/Rat, Monkey or Rooster; Libra/Tiger and Monkey, or Aquarius/Rat and Monkey. These are your allies. Now for your detractors: all of them Dogs of the Gemini, Virgo and Pisces persuasions. Now that wasn't so hard, was it?

Home and Family

Luxury doesn't come first for the Sagittarius/Dragon. But status does. The Sagittarius born under the sign of Dragon will not be likely to hang his coat of arms over a door in just any old part of town. This subject wants to live in the "best" neighborhood, send his or her kids to the "right" schools, and will be sure to shop in all the "finest" emporia. Pared-down opulence and originality will characterize the abode of Sagittarius/Dragon. "Let's turn the attic into an office and tear up the bathroom tile and put in an aquarium." Sagittarius/Dragon likes to do things with imagination and style.

The Sagittarius/Dragon is a born parent. This person leads well and takes responsibility seriously. Moreover, parenting and protecting, nurturing and looking after others gives the Dragon born Sagittarius real personal gratification. He or she will be firm and insist kids stay close to the family circle while growing up. No child will be made to feel insecure so long as he has a Sagittarius/Dragon for a Mom or Dad. These folks are notorious for taking care of their own. They pile everybody in the car and leave on vacation as a gang, pack picnic lunches, and hike up the mountainside along with the best of them.

As a child this person will probably be bubbly and enthusiastic. She will invariably get involved in group projects of which she is the chief. These kids are usually popular with school friends and playmates. Teachers appreciate their willingness to lead, but may sometimes feel a shade threatened by the Sagittarius/Dragon's sense of superiority. There is nothing this child feels he or she cannot accomplish, so sometimes they are sorely disappointed in themselves. You can talk to them directly and not fear breaking their spirit; these little people are tough and capable. They should be taught patience.

Profession

What a Dragon born in Sagittarius sets out to do, he means to see accomplished. This person manifestly wants what he wants when he wants it. Now, obviously this self-belief has its drawbacks. Nobody is invincible, least of all the most sentimental Dragon of them all, Sagittarius. But that deeply emotional foible is precisely what makes him or her so charming. Many of the Sagittarian Dragon's battles are inadvertently won by virtue of this happy personality quirk. What looks like a rock is actually a marshmallow. But as it talks and acts like a rock, nobody can tell the difference. Tricky, no?

The Sagittarius/Dragon will probably not want to play any game where he or she is not the leader. This is a beloved boss, a person who commands great respect from employees and associates. Another cleverness of this combined sign is that he or she knows when to stand back and let events take over. This character can be hasty but is sometimes surprisingly wise as well.

Careers that suit this person are: nursery school director, bookstore owner, TV producer, insurance magnate, banker, entrepreneur, builder, politician, senator, lawyer, theologian, business consultant, writer, editor, publisher.

Some famous Sagittarius/Dragons: Louisa May Alcott, Betty Grable, Richard Pryor, Bruce Lee, Chuck Mangione, Frank Zappa, Francisco Franco, Robert Laffont, Zachary Taylor.

SAGITTARIUS

CHEERFULNESS	OUTSPOKENNESS
OPENHANDEDNESS	RECKLESSNESS
SOLICITUDE	BAD MANNERS
VALOR	VACILLATION
HONOR	CARELESSNESS
REASON	CONTRADICTION

"I see"

Fire, Jupiter, Mutable

SNAKE

INTUITION	DISSIMULATION
ATTRACTIVENESS	EXTRAVAGANCE
DISCRETION	LAZINESS
SAGACITY	CUPIDITY
CLAIRVOYANCE	PRESUMPTION
COMPASSION	EXCLUSIVENESS

"I sense"

Negative Fire, Yang

Solicitude personified, the Sagittarius/Snake cares for those he loves and admires, and looks after everything from home to car interior with a sense of concern that makes Florence Nightingale look like a slouch. This is a creature of dignity and bearing whose manners and taste for refinement are second only to an unparalleled devotion to virtue. The Sagittarian Snake is a human luxury item, without the expensive price tag.

This character is never noisy or boisterous. Yet much gets said. The Sagittarius/Snake waves no banners, makes no waves. Yet he is zealously involved in championing causes. This person keeps his counsel and recoils before conflict. Yet he communicates expertly, untangles complex arguments, and just about never loses an inning.

Thing is, people born in this combination of signs are singularly motivated to rise above their station or birthright. The average successful Sagittarius/Snake is someone who has started small and known how to slither up and through the ranks without hue or cry because he or she wanted a better life. This person is an idealist. He or she is pure of heart and straightforward, yet discreet.

To the Snake born in Sagittarius, the act of exerting oneself is visible proof of moral rectitude. Unlike so many of their serpentine counterparts, Sagittarius/Snakes are not lazy, and sincerely do not mind getting up to fetch you that drink or going out in the snow to run four miles a day. In their quiet way, these people are powerhouses of energy. As they are stealthy and never seem in a hurry, you would never guess at their efficiency. But what they can accomplish in one day without a sound or a hair out of place is astounding.

Too, Sagittarius/Snakes are organizational wizards. Give them a broken-down office structure or an unruly bunch of children for a few days and they will put everything to rights. Their manner is never splashy or harsh. But the firm set of their mouths tells you that these pristine characters don't fool around. When it comes to getting the basement cleaned, watch their style.

Sagittarius/Snakes are not ones to take risks. They are neither cowardly nor fearful. They like sports and practice everything from skiing to skydiving without a second's hesitation. But they don't go around jousting with danger or looking for adventure in speleology or big game hunting. Similarly, in their daily life, Sagittarius/Snakes don't go tempting the devil. They are wont to enjoy the comforts of a good thing, and readily know when they have caught one by the tail.

The Snake born in Sagittarius doesn't meddle. He will not gossip or mix in affairs that don't directly involve him. These people are curious enough, but will not go out of their way to uncover someone's motives. They are not uninterested in the business of others, but they are by nature judicious. The Sagittarius/Snake feels that each of us has carved out a niche in life and that he likes his just fine. He hopes you are also comfy in yours, but he will probably not pry far enough to find out.

Love

Sagittarians often marry late. Sagittarius/Snakes sometimes don't marry at all. They do tend, however, to enjoy a few high-quality long-term relationships of a profound and intimate type. Often, Sagittarius/Snakes engage lovers and/or mates in long, serious discussions. They have a confidential air about them that awakens the snoop in some. "What can he be thinking?" one may wonder. "Such a strong silent type," others may remark. When they are in love, Sagittarian Snakes exhibit amazing dedication. They are usually faithful because to be promiscuous would strike them as vulgar and superficial.

If you love one of these classy types I advise you to clean up your act fast. If you want to keep the Sagittarius/Snake in the style to which he has accustomed himself, you will have to learn how to live quietly and elegantly, never to raise your voice and even learn how to jog and stay on a diet. Wisdom above all is the Sagittarius/Snake's motto. Carelessness offends his sensibilities. So be cool and don't show your hand. The Sagittarius/Snake loves mystery,

Compatibilities

Affiliations with Oxen of the Leo, Libra and Aquarius schools will be positive and engender prosperity. You'll also establish complicity with Aries and Aquarius/Roosters. Such relationships flourish best in urban environments. Virgos, Geminis and Pisceans are not your favorite people, particularly Gemini/Monkey, Virgo/Tiger and Pig, and Pisces/Tiger, Monkey and Pig natives.

Home and Family

This person's home will be first, last and always attractive. The basis of his or her lifestyle is peacefulness and a constant quest for refinement. The Sagittarius/Snake will prefer antiques to modern furnishings. He or she will go in for the real thing in jewelry, paintings, and even in roofing and siding. The Sagittarius/Snake is an authenticity freak. He pursues the truth right down to the last mohair on his overcoat. She only wears cashmere sweaters if she can help it. With Sagittarius/Snake, it's no glitz all the way.

This person will make a fabulously creative and interested parent. The comforts of home will be offered little Georgie and Lisa by the dozen. Each child will be carefully followed by everybody, from allergists to pierced-ear specialists. Perhaps the Sagittarius/Snake can be accused of "overhothousing" his or her kids. The bathtub doesn't really have to be scrubbed with a velvet sponge after each use, does it? Seriously, children are extemporaneous at best; let them take risks even if they break a bone or two. It helps them learn about life outside the greenhouse.

A baby Sagittarius/Snake will show early signs of meticulousness, and suffer enormously from discord and household disruptions. This child needs a quiet intellectual environment and plenty of countrified experience to ease him into the future. He or she will be outgoing and loving toward other kids. Also, parent-pleasing is a by-product of this kid's whole persona. The little Sagittarius/Snake wants his folks to be proud of him or her. They will bend over backwards to make a sad Mom or Dad smile.

Profession

All jobs that require caring for others are suitable for this solid citizen type. He or she will naturally prefer careers that allow for dealing with people, organizing or solving sticky human problems. Paperwork doesn't annoy the Sagittarius/Snake outrageously, and he or she works well in all areas demanding attention to detail.

The Sagittarius/Snake makes an excellent, sane, and quiet-spoken boss. He or she will endeavor to be just in all delegation of labor, and will probably not play favorites. This person is a model employee. As long as their hair doesn't get too messed up or their personal routine disrupted, Sagittarius/Snakes move along smoothly and rarely balk. This person makes an excellent entrepreneur, as he or she will be a self-starter—and finisher!

Jobs that best suit the Sagittarius/Snake are: maître d'hotel, hostess, physician, nurse, philosopher, psychiatrist, decorator, surgeon, dentist, gardener, florist, dog trainer, astrologer, researcher, chef, shepherd.

Some famous Sagittarius/Snakes: Pope John XXIII, Munro Leaf, Ossie Davis, Howard Hughes, Antoine de Caunes, Beau Bridges, Claude Terrail, Dionne Warwick, Eddie Rabbit, Francis Cabrel, John Davidson, Leslie Stahl, Pierre Brasseur.

SAGITTARIUS

HORSE

CHEERFULNESS	OUTSPOKENNESS	PERSUASIVENESS	SELFISHNESS
OPENHANDEDNESS	RECKLESSNESS	UNSCRUPULOUSNESS	AUTONOMY
SOLICITUDE	BAD MANNERS	POPULARITY	REBELLION
VALOR	VACILLATION	STYLE	HASTE
HONOR	CARELESSNESS	DEXTERITY	ANXIETY
REASON	CONTRADICTION	ACCOMPLISHMEN	PRAGMATISM

"I see"

Fire, Jupiter, Mutable

"I demand"

Positive Fire, Yang

A great striding Horse figure, the Sagittarius/Horse is three-quarters Horse and only one part man. As they say in westerns, "That's a lot of horse!" Interestingly, this person is more head than beast. The Sagittarian born Horse operates first out of homespun values, next in search of self-control, and thirdly he concentrates on finding and achieving a goal.

Sagittarius/Horses are never tired. Black circles under their eyes, facial features dragging on the sidewalk and skin the color of pigeon feathers mean nothing to this veritable generator of a person. "You must be exhausted," one says after they have stayed up three days and nights working on a schedule that would have long since silenced Brazil. The Sagittarius/Horse glances at you as though you'd asked her her name. "Me? Tired? Never!" And it's true. These people work until they drop.

The Sagittarius/Horse has good manners. These develop quite naturally through the years because Sagittarian Horses are concerned with social graces and involve themselves readily in matters of social class. I won't say the Sagittarian born Horse is a snob, but almost. In any case, he or she is a person who longs to be set apart from the horde. Sagittarius/Horse takes pleasure in being different.

Born under this dual sign of caring and pragmatism, the Sagittarius/Horse subject represents the perfect blend of these two qualities. He or she will take up causes and go for broke on committees the way Sagittarians do, but they will only sacrifice their time to such "isms" and beliefs that they expect to have feasible outcomes. These people are too practical to dream the utterly impossible dream.

The Horse born in Sagittarius wants to be the star of his or her own life. They are not particularly attracted by worldly celebrity, but rather forge ahead for the purpose of gaining self-respect through their success. The Sagittarius/Horse has high ideals for himself, for his work and for the work of those close to him. Pleasure is important only insofar as it gives release from tension and anxiety, and in that way increases productivity in work. This Horse will be the pivotal element in his home or workplace; those who circulate around him or her will do so by virtue of the Sagittarius/Horse's generosity of both spirit and pocketbook.

If poverty could bring the Sagittarius/Horse happiness and freedom from worry, I don't think he would mind being without money. But this is a person who requires a solid framework where he feels in control. Frameworks don't come cheap these days. Somebody has to pay the rent and insurance, utilities and cleaning people. For this reason penury threatens the well-being of Sagittarius/Horse. His security comes from without. So it must be bought.

The Sagittarius/Horse may seem marginal to some. He or she sometimes has outrageous notions. Thing is, their type of nonconformity is only strange and outlandish insofar as it reflects off something more traditional. Hence the Sagittarius/Horse may seem weird and unusual sometimes, but his style of weirdness is dependent on the contrast to society's humdrum. Sagittarius/Horses are not so bohemian as to become hermits or poets who move to remote places and avoid all worldly contact. They are so tempted to put in their two cents that they cannot remain forever out of the mainstream.

Early recklessness can prompt unwise judgments. But the Sagittarius/Horse grows wiser with age. He soon learns how to keep his word, to provide and care for family and close collaborators, to stand quietly back waiting for the right opportunity. Galloping is for kids. Life, according to the mature Sagittarius/Horse, should be lived at a pleasant canter, never too fast and never too slow, but always going in the same direction—forward.

Love

Early on, the Sagittarius/Horse will make at least one or two false moves in romance. This character is born ardent. His wild oats are plentiful. But when age creeps up, the Sagittarius/Horse learns to control his or her beastly side and seeks a partner who can fit into the framework of which I spoke earlier.

Sagittarius/Horse does not want a namby-pamby, obedient partner who never questions her opinions. But he may want someone to look after the details of home and family while Sagittarius is busy providing for everybody's porridge. Above all, this person wants no interference, and prefers to make it clear from day one that love is serious business for him or her. Hanky-panky will be excluded in favor of application of fanny to seat of chair or nose to grindstone.

If you care for a Sagittarius/Horse, don't get hung up on him or her. Be your own person. Represent a mental challenge. Play a little hard to get. But don't ever think you will turn this autonomous person around to your way of living. It is you who will have to learn to get up at five A.M. and let the cat in, make the coffee, and pack Sagittarius/Horse's suitcase for a trip to Dallas. And where is the Sagittarius/Horse all this time? On the phone to Bonn or Rome or London, jabbering on about deals and plans and more deals. Sagittarius/Horse's mission comes first. Whatever yours is will automatically be less important.

Compatibilities

With your drive for personal success, you'll be needing a patient, serious partner to share your life. Take a mate from Aries, Libra, Leo or Aquarius, who was hatched in a Tiger year. Or better still, if you can trap one, get an Aries, Leo or Libra/Goat. They are ever so much more patient with your comings and goings. A Libra or Aquarius/Dog will stand by you through thick and thin, too. Contrarily, I advise you against Virgo, Gemini or Pisces/ Rats.

Home and Family

The homes of Sagittarians born in Horse years are either somebody else's rented taste, and decor or, at best, decorated by their mate. The only part of his home that really interests the Sagittarius/Horse is the work area. It can be a den or a basement tool room or atelier or studio or office or utility room, but it must be all his own. Here, the stamp of equine practicality will shine. High tech is an understatement: track lighting, and Formica desks with large-surfaced tops, and computer terminals galore! The rest? Those couches you wanted from Roche et Bobois... all right, sure, buy them. Sagittarius/Horse is generous but he or she is not up to paying attention to fripfrap. Clothes will follow the same pattern: comfortable and classical with the odd departure from beige and navy blue into gray flannel. Yellow? Only for costume balls.

The Sagittarius/Horse parent provides. Kids will be seen and even heard, but Mom or Dad Sagittarius/Horse may not have scads of time to play tiddlywinks with them. These are busy, energetic parents whose athletic talents are reserved for their own sports interests and who, anyway, have a bit of difficulty stooping to crawling on the floor with toddlers. Noblesse prevents.

As a child this person will be talented for all sports activities. Teachers may accuse the Sagittarian Horse of adding fantasy to her work. This is the kid who repeatedly draws pictures of her dog in the margin of her math papers. It doesn't occur to the teacher that maybe she's bored out of her mind. Instead this kid is often scolded for daydreaming.

At home this child will be obedient and loving. He or she wants to be included in all activities and may even seek to take over the management of group efforts. Frankly, the Sagittarius/Horse wouldn't mind being an only child. These people love control.

Profession

This person's talents lie in areas requiring insight and a keen sense of observation and caring. All careers involving people and their trials and tribulations will suit the Sagittarius/Horse. They are gifted for organization and management. They have natural presence and poise and know how to meet the public. Bossing comes naturally to this leader type. But the Sagittarius/ Horse is not classically bossy. He or she will be directive and mutely authoritarian. A smile always accompanies an order or request.

The Sagittarius/Horse makes a terrific employee, too. They are serious and responsible people who care about getting ahead. What more could any employer want? As for working alone, the Sagittarius/Horse can be a creative self-starter, but he prefers working in groups to functioning alone.

Some suitable careers for Sagittarius/Horses are: physical education teacher, cattle rancher, real estate developer, writer, diplomat, golf pro, football coach, actor, actress, journalist, market analyst, politician, orchestra leader, psychiatrist.

Famous Sagittarius/Horses: Leonid Brezhnev, James Thurber, Alexander Solzhenitsyn, Jean-Luc Godard, Jimi Hendrix, Jean-Louis Trintignant, Andy Williams, Bob Guccione, Buck Henry, G. Gordon Liddy, Maximilian Schell, Pierre Desgraupes.

SAGITTARIUS

GOAT

CHEERFULNESS	OUTSPOKENNESS	INVENTION	PARASITISM
OPENHANDEDNESS	RECKLESSNESS	LACK OF FORESIGHT	SENSITIVITY
SOLICITUDE	BAD MANNERS	PERSEVERANCE	TARDINESS
VALOR	VACILLATION	WHIMSY	PESSIMISM
HONOR	CARELESSNESS	GOOD MANNERS	TASTE
REASON	CONTRADICTION	IMPRACTICALITY	WORRY

"I see"

Fire, Jupiter, Mutable

"I depend"

Negative Fire, Yang

Sagittarius/Goat enjoys a giant creativity. Invention and enterprise are second nature to this dynamic, clear-thinking soul. Yet, there is one rub. Goats only function well when they feel secure. Lack of means or the threat of financial ruin, family schisms and personal jeopardies of all sorts will flummox this Goat and throw him off his feed. The major struggle for this valiant and courageous character will revolve around getting and keeping protection for himself and family and friends.

The Goat personality, with its built-in grace and charm, brings mannerliness and a taste for style to the sometimes overly rustic Sagittarius. In the case of this double sign, the Sagittarian gets to keep all of his solicitous instincts and shows great willingness to help others. But this Goatly Sagittarius is not recklessly or interferingly helpful. This Goat has finely tuned antennae that tell him when he is needed. Then, in a wink, he hops in the driver's seat and dashes to rescue the fair maiden in distress. Sagittarian Goats have solutions for all your problems. They may suggest weirdo answers to dilemmas you would never dream up in a lifetime of cogitating. Or they may simply take your problem home with them and unravel it at their ease until three in the morning.

Time and schedules, hours for work and hours for play, and so on don't mean anything to Sagittarius/Goats. They are relatively prompt as they care for and are polite to others. But chunks of organized time don't really exist in the minds of these altruistic creators. Sagittarius/Goats like to catnap between four and six A.M., get up and drive through from California to Florida, and then go to sleep for three straight days. If she needs to sleep, she will. But in the meantime, more important, is the project, the enterprise, the venture at hand. When that's done they can rest. Not before.

And with these perseverant innovators, whose enthusiasm for detail and works of great intricacy is dauntless and whose creativity is boundless, there is always another endeavor in the wind. Don't look now, but that Sagittarius/Goat who just finished building her own ten-room house from scratch out of non-returnable soda bottles is about to embark on a study trip to Tibet. Of course, she won't leave until she has directed a new musical comedy show for the church benefit and installed her own central heating system. The Sagittarius/Goat is indefatigably constructive.

The Sagittarius/Goat is also a good judge of usefulness. He or she will be able to tell right off if a new lighting system or a pair of sawhorses will serve a defined purpose. These people have a good memory for detail, and yet sometimes slack off when it comes to attending to them. Final touches are not the province of the Goat born in Sagittarius. He or she will be happy to think up the plot and work out the architecture and even draw you a plan for your next book, but when it comes to correcting spelling errors, they want someone else to take over. Their business is imagination.

Sometimes, because these people are so specifically conception-oriented, they come up with impractical schemes. There is not just one unfinished project in this subject's closet, there are thirty-one. Some plans just don't pan out. Sagittarius/Goats never cry over spilt effort. They'd sooner think up some new earth-shaking device and go about gathering parts to put that together.

Love

Oddly circumspect in love relations, the Sagittarius/Goat doesn't fit into the child bride or groom category. As we already know, the Goat must have security. Without it, he flails and flounders and flubs. So until this person has amassed sufficient means and sorted out enough of life's daily problems to suit his or her need for self-safety, he will not be likely to take on the responsibility of someone else. This person has an independent streak where love is concerned, too, and doesn't want to be held down or limited in any way. Freedom is almost as important to the Sagittarius Goat as love.

If you love a Sagittarius/Goat person, you will certainly esteem him first. These inventive, interesting folks can always boast admirers by the dozen.

They are mostly faithful in love affairs, as they are usually too busy with their projects to go bird-dogging. Besides, they have enough to worry about with one person to help and care for and drive and be interrupted by. You will best serve this character by learning how to take care of details he or she eschews. If you cook and clean as well, you can very quickly render yourself indispensable. The Sagittarian Goat sometimes forgets to eat, and dirty dishes are his or her constant companion. Tiptoe a lot. Genius at work.

Compatibilities

Liaison is readily established between you and members of the Aries, Libra and Aquarius/Cat set. Leo, Libra and Aquarius/Pigs make excellent mates for you. They encourage your creative side. For some extra action, try an Aries/Horse. They inspire your admiration. A Gemini, Virgo or Pisces/Dog person will nag you and drive you to drink. Stay out of the way of Gemini/ Tigers, and Virgo and Pisces/Oxen too.

Home and Family

If possible, this person will invariably choose to live in the countryside. Cities, with their noise and clatter, get in the way of the Sagittarius/Goat's calm center. This character is attracted by solitude and silence. Starry nights tranquilize him. Thunder and lightning excite his poetic spirit. Sagittarius/ Goats need the proximity of the elements to help them restoke furnaces of energy depleted by the inhuman efforts for which they are so famous. So the Sagittarius/Goat's house may not be fancy, but it will surely be solid and comfortable, and as isolated as possible.

This person makes a terrific parent. He or she really cares for children and is interested in what makes them tick. The Sagittarius/Goat likes the way kids' minds work, and admires childlike spontaneity and verve. The Sagittarius/ Goat, despite his advanced creative mind, will not be a permissive parent. Instead, this person's kids will be called upon to be courteous and curious. Sagittarius/ Goat is progressive, however. He or she works alongside kids to teach them crafts or help them with school projects.

The Sagittarius/Goat child is removed from the group vector by virtue of his exceptional views. This little person may feel "out of it" a lot of the time, and suffer from loneliness in a crowd. Parents are well advised to encourage this child in creative pursuits, providing lessons and tutors where possible. There is often real genius in this child's mind. But insecurity is the enemy of that spark. All family disruptions and parental discord upset this sensitive kid's nerves. He or she takes everything to heart and wants to help to make it better. Protect this child if you can.

Profession

Ordinarily Goat subjects suffer from lack of foresight. They are the people who buy one quart of milk for a set of hungry sextuplets. But here Sagittarius, with his drive to change the future, is heeded by the Goat, so Sagittarius/Goats are rather careful souls. They are family-oriented and security-minded and thus less dependent or parasitic than many other Goat natives. They have a keen eye for social commentary. They are cooperative in the extreme, and certainly not afraid of hard labor—on their own terms, of course. They often know how to turn a little bit of wealth into a lot of money.

The Sagittarius/Goat boss is well loved by employees. He or she may be criticized for not being harsh enough. But the Sagittarius born Goat rules by sweetness. His orders are sugarcoated and the results are sometimes not half bad. If he is employed in a lucrative job he will be greatly appreciated by superiors. Sagittarius/Goats are a great addition to any office situation. They are good at jobs requiring individual effort and offering personal gain. The Sagittarius/Goat cares what others think and always tries to please.

Careers that may fit into the Sagittarius/Goat's life are: psychiatrist, insurance agent, artist (all sorts), house painter, choreographer, wine grower, doctor, lawyer, missionary, farmer, designer, musician, teacher, clergyman, seamstress, picture framer.

Famous Sagittarius/Goats: Jane Austen, Mark Twain, Andrew Carnegie, Anna Freud, Alberto Moravia, Busby Berkeley, Randy Newman, Bill Wilson, Billie Jean King, Georges Seurat, Jim Morrison, Michael Owen, Rita Moreno.

SAGITTARIUS

CHEERFULNESS	OUTSPOKENNESS
OPENHANDEDNESS	RECKLESSNESS
SOLICITUDE	BAD MANNERS
VALOR	VACILLATION
HONOR	CARELESSNESS
REASON	CONTRADICTION

"I see"

Fire, Jupiter, Mutable

MONKEY

IMPROVISATION	DECEIT
CUNNING	RUSE
STABILITY	LOQUACITY
SELF-INVOLVEMENT	LEADERS
WIT	SILLINESS
OPPORTUNISM	ZEAL

"I plan"

Positive Metal, Yin

Sagittarians are always freethinkers. They blaze trails and shoot for the future. They are glib and humanitarian. They are direct and cheerful. Much of the above description also fits the Monkey character. So, in some ways, the Sagittarian Monkey is in harmony with both sides of his nature. His outgoing side doesn't have to do daily battle with some introverted tendency to hide under rocks when company comes. Sagittarius/Monkey is comfortable in his skin.

But a basic rift exists between the Sagittarian and his Monkey counterpart. Sagittarians are altruistic and other-oriented. Sagittarians are truthful and like to play daredevil. The Monkey is not a bit like that. The Monkey is cunning itself, careful never to be too direct, and capable of epic feats of circuitousness. He rarely tempts the devil unless he knows he can beat him, and his orientation is toward himself rather than toward others.

So what happens? Well, it's quite simple. Monkey turns Sagittarius into a natural leader. This person has the necessary ardor and force to move a mountain, and he also possesses the guile and opportunism needed to establish his own government on the same site. Sagittarius/Monkeys take over. They like to run things and make decisions and order people around and make laws and initiate changes and make alterations. And before you can say "Sagittarius/Monkey" this tricky little number is having a street named after himself—and while he's at it, maybe he'll name one after his girlfriend, too.

Huge efforts don't bother the Sagittarius/Monkey either. These capable people are organized and go right to the heart of any given problem. They are earnest and believe fervently in their creeds and ideals. They are attractive. And they are very convincing. Sagittarius/Monkeys naturally love to speak in public and debate prickly subjects with aplomb and common sense. They like money and know how to spend it wisely and generously.

Silliness, for the Monkey born in Sagittarius, will be reserved for private parties. The public image of this power-seeking dynamo will be grave. Sagittarius/Monkey wants to be taken seriously. With friends or intimates this character may be a perfect clown, dancing on tables and enlivening gatherings with witty comments and crazy antics. But image-wise, this bright person is nobody's fool.

Sagittarius/Monkeys think big. They never putter around with small potatoes. These folks are interested in gain and authority. They are excellent administrators and just about never enter into direct conflict. These people are essentially conservative, and even if they have a streak of the liberal in them, they will be careful to cloak it in middle-of-the-road clothing. Monkeys born in Sagittarius like hefty challenges. They are expert at public relations. They are their own best ambassadors and seem to know instinctively how to gently sway public opinion in their own favor.

Love

Sagittarius/Monkeys are a bit uncomfortable in intimacy. They don't give easily of their emotions, and tend to shrink from the bonds that coupledom imposes. The Sagittarius/Monkey will be hesitant about marrying or hitching up with someone for life. This character sees beyond each relationship, and wonders whether or not in a few years' time she will become bored with the loved one. There is a refusal in this character to take on emotional responsibility for anything other than his missions. He will be fun to hang around with but I'm not sure I'd want him to marry my sister.

If you are attracted to the challenging Sagittarius/Monkey, use wiles to fight wiles. Don't be too declarative or easy for this person to bag. Otherwise, he will lose interest overnight. You will best charm this difficult subject by challenging her mind, testing her mettle and taking little trips by yourself from time to time just to keep her on her toes. For heaven's sake, don't say you are only going to the neighboring village. Pretend you've been called away on affairs of state.

Compatibilities

Aries, Libra and Aquarius/Rats spur you to greater heights. You'll not be sorry for taking up with Leo, Libra or Aquarius/Dragons either. There's no future for you with Virgo, Gemini or Pisces/Pigs. Gemini and Pisces/Oxen demand far too much stability for your taste. And Virgos of both the Cat and Tiger persuasions prevent you from advancing on your own terms. Pisces/Snakes are lovely. But you can't have one. It just won't work.

Home and Family

This person's interior will be practical and sensible. He will probably own a number of objets d'art picked up in his many travels. But there is not much showiness in the Sagittarius/Monkey's taste. He or she does not want to impress through furnishings. A comfortable and well-organized, functional home is this person's aim. The Sagittarius/Monkey's wardrobe will be publicly bourgeois old-line and privately casual.

The Sagittarius/Monkey is not apt to marry young and have a slew of stair-step babies trotting around underfoot by age twenty-five. No. This person has personal advancement in mind before everything else. Then, once he or she is established in a solid career, it will be time enough for making babies. And one or two will suffice, thank you. Sagittarian Monkeys will be careful parents who provide handsomely for their children's futures. They are concerned with public appearances and will make their children behave.

If you have a Sagittarius/Monkey child, you have probably already noticed how serious he or she threatens to become. Although at home these little kids can be very rough-and-tumble, they can usually contain themselves in school. This child will have talent for organization and leadership. They can benefit from early training in public speaking or theater work. They are sensitive but private about their emotions. It's rather difficult to know what they are thinking. Never pry. Question gently.

Profession

The Sagittarius/Monkey rarely takes the path of least resistance. He or she will be, adept at managing and has great organizational acumen. These people are problem solvers. They see concrete solutions to puzzles that stymie whole commissions of specialists. "Why don't we turn it into a stadium then?" they will suggest at the town planning board meeting. "We can make it profitable by building a parking lot underneath."

The Sagittarius/Monkey always has an answer. And if he doesn't know what he's yammering about—it certainly sounds as if he does. Of course this person is a leader and will want to boss. The Sagittarian Monkey is not sarcastic or mean to his subordinates. But he does sometimes have a blustery way of acting superior that gets under the skin of employees. Largely, he can be trusted to take over in all areas requiring common-sense administration. This person doesn't stay an underling for long, but he or she knows how to be flexible for promotional purposes and cooperative for gain. These folks work very well alone.

Careers that suit the Sagittarius/Monkey are: politician, writer, ambassador, office manager, account executive, lobbyist, negotiator, personnel director, economist.

Famous Sagittarius/Monkeys: John Milton, Claude Levi-Strauss, Ellen Burstyn, Larry Bird, Anna Shlumsky, Christina Aguilera, Claire Chazal, Dave Brubeck, Enrio Macias, Jacques Chirac, Ric Felix, Ricardo Montalban.

The New Astrology

SAGITTARIUS

CHEERFULNESS	OUTSPOKENNESS
OPENHANDEDNESS	RECKLESSNESS
SOLICITUDE	BAD MANNERS
VALOR	VACILLATION
HONOR	CARELESSNESS
REASON	CONTRADICTION

"I see"

Fire, Jupiter, Mutable

ROOSTER

RESILIENCE	COCKINESS
ENTHUSIASM	BOASTFULNESS
CANDOR	BLIND FAITH
CONSERVATISM	PEDANTRY
CHIC	BOSSINESS
HUMOR	DISSIPATION

"I overcome"

Negative Metal, Yang

Buoyancy characterizes the Sagittarian Rooster. He's atwitter with chitchat and agog with stories of adventure. This subject, born under two of the most high-strung signs, will be nervous, frank, candid, and a bit carried away with himself. The word is enthusiasm but it's more than that. Sagittarius/Roosters are full of dash and élan. They cut an impressive figure wherever they go— and they go everywhere!

Despite the Sagittarius/Rooster's determination to cover half the globe by age thirteen, this person is deep-down sensible and lives far more carefully than the impression implies. He or she will have noble aims. They entertain a kind of Robin Hood objective to rob from the rich and give to the poor. Not that Sagittarius/Roosters are thieves. There is no evidence to that effect. But they can be secret pirates, leering at those ships that pass in the night loaded with jewels and furs yet denying themselves chicanery. The Sagittarian Rooster is a lover of truth. He deplores phoniness.

Sagittarius/Roosters are beset by their noble aims at a very young age. They would like to "do good" in the old-fashioned missionary sense. They may travel to Africa or India to help poor people, or they may stay closer to home and hire on as listeners in a suicide center. But whatever they undertake is often disappointing to their starkly honest natures. No charity can be perfect. There's always a hitch. Somebody has a hand in the till or funds are being misused or poor people in some distant land refuse help for religious reasons. Philanthropy is mined with disappointment.

For this reason, the Sagittarius/Rooster is often seen as disenchanted, locked in an ideal that won't let him or her loose, but that doesn't work either. For some less resilient souls this sort of disillusion could lead to dejection and even self-pity. But not for the Sagittarius/Rooster. In a matter of days you will find this character back on his feet, packing a suitcase for yet another foray into the wilds of humanitarianism. It's the old story: You can't keep a good man down.

Withal, the Sagittarius/Rooster has fairly good sense. He only seems reckless and acts boasting and cocky. Underneath, this person has his eye on the needle at all times and is monitoring his own progress critically. These people realize that freedom and adventure are too attractive to them, and know that one day they must settle down or become patently ridiculous. When that day comes, Sagittarius/Roosters land themselves cushy jobs with serious titles on the doors, or simply sit down and start writing books about their many exploits.

Sagittarius/Roosters have good manners, yet sometimes they can be snappy and brusque. A harsh remark in the midst of a seemingly ordinary calm conversation is not unusual coming from these people. They are brutally frank. They thrive on adversity and challenge. They are not afraid to stoop to conquer, and they care greatly for friends and family. In fact, I would say that no matter where this person journeys in a lifetime, he or she will remain forever tied to duty and responsibility at home, a free spirit locked in the body of a dutiful do-gooder. Maybe that's why Sagittarius/Roosters are always departing and leaving the barnyard door ajar, so they can return to their favorite prison when the chips are down.

Love

Sagittarius/Roosters are not always lucky in love. They are by turns too demanding or too docile. In love affairs there is always a delicate gray area of deceit. Some things are better not discussed when it comes to passions and jealousies. Well, the Sagittarius/Rooster can't hack the deceit part. He or she wants all the cards on the table and no double-dealing. Moreover, as this person is so indomitable and fiercely dynamic, he or she often takes up with someone who needs help, someone whose aims are not fixed, and who seems so adorably lost. This is what I call the Sagittarius "Popeye" complex. Good Samaritan time. Of course, pity is not love. But sometimes Sagittarius/ Roosters can't tell the difference.

If you love a Sagittarius/Rooster, try to jolly her out of a rigid sense of duty by tickling or amusing her in some fashion. Take him to the theater and buy him pop-up toys. Get these people out of their duty rut, And most of all, don't take advantage of this person's kindly, caring nature. A hurt Sagittarius/Rooster is not a pretty sight.

Compatibilities

Aries Leo, Libra and Aquarius/Snakes find you irresistible, and the feeling is mutual. Leo, Libra and Aquarius/Oxen provide you with both pleasure and safety from harm. And the real joys of romance arrive in the form of Leo and/or Libra/Dragons. They are so-o-o-o-o impressive. Virgo and Gemini/Rooster subjects are no fun for you to keep around. Pisces/Dogs drive you mad with their incessant worrying, and Virgo and Pisces/Cats are far too bossy and unadventurous for you to put up with them for long.

Home and Family

The Sagittarius/Rooster's home will be spare yet elegant. Comfort is not the primary goal. Appearance and attractiveness come first. Having a "good address" helps, too. Not that Sagittarius/Rooster is a snob—far from it. But this person is essentially conservative, prefers security to danger, and cannot tolerate messiness or disorder. So the Sagittarius/Rooster often sets up shop in a reputable area. He or she is gone much of the time so "home" is a dubious term at best to describe Sagittarius/Rooster digs.

This person would love to be a parent. But where to find the time? They have their Indians in Bolivia, their Puerto Ricans in Harlem and their immigrants in Texas to attend to first. After that, they have to hurry home to spend Christmas with the folks and buy all those toys for the nieces and nephews. And if Sagittarius/Rooster does settle down, how will he or she ever get free again to go trotting off to Brazil? The subject of children is a tricky one for the Sagittarian born Rooster. It's yes and no and yes and no until one day it seems impossible. Sagittarius/Rooster is too peripatetic to be a parent.

The Sagittarius/Rooster child will play at adventurous games. You may try to interest him or her in piano lessons or needlepoint, but it probably won't take. And if it does, it's because this kid is wholeheartedly dutiful and doesn't want to hurt parents' feelings. This child is a maverick. He may not get along well in the confined ambience of a schoolroom. She's always dreaming of becoming a famous ballerina who gives all her money to the poor. They will stick out education if parents make it clear there is no other route. Otherwise, the Sagittarius/Rooster is likely to go far away from home in an attempt to find himself in the eyes of strangers.

Profession

All careers involving movement and travel suit this person. Sagittarian Roosters are talkative and frequently never shut up in three languages. They have a natural ability to sort out details, are visionary about future trends and tuned in to fashions. The Sagittarius born Rooster seeks to have a cosmic view of his environment and indeed of the whole universe. He's got good sense and doesn't hesitate before making decisions. Sagittarius/Roosters get on with things. Born bossy, the Sagittarius/Rooster nonetheless is not sure if he wants that top job all that much. If he agrees to be the chief in Chicago, then what will happen to the Indians in the Andes? The answer is a job where Sagittarius/Rooster travels a lot and gets to see a lot of progress in a short time. As an employee, this person is happy as long as he sees a light at the end of the tunnel—a promotion to tour guide, for example.

Jobs that may please the Sagittarius/Rooster are: photographer for National Geographic, UNESCO or peace corps volunteer, publisher of travel books, writer, performer, journalist, geologist, cartographer, doctor, missionary, roadie, pirate, prospector, logger, travel agent.

Some famous Sagittarius/Roosters: Deanna Durbin, Tim Conway, Flip Wilson, Bernard Haller, Britney Spears, Caroline Kennedy, François de Closets.

SAGITTARIUS		DOG	

CHEERFULNESS	OUTSPOKENNESS	CONSTANCY	UNEASINES
OPENHANDEDNESS	RECKLESSNESS	UNSOCIABILITY	CRITICISM
SOLICITUDE	BAD MANNERS	RESPECTABILITY	DUTY
VALOR	VACILLATION	SELF-RIGHTEOUSNESS	CYNICISM
HONOR	CARELESSNESS	INTELLIGENCE	HEROISM
REASON	CONTRADICTION	TACTLESSNESS	MORALITY

"I see"

Fire, Jupiter, Mutable

"I worry"

Positive Metal, Yang

The dry hero that is Sagittarius/Dog embodies all of the Sagittarian's idealist traits, the adventurousness, the future vision, the bravura and the fire. But this person also takes on those creditable qualities native to all born under the sign of the Dog: honor and sincerity, loyalty and respectability. Both signs are endowed with a loose tongue. Sagittarians like to be frank and to expound. Dogs, although circumspect and mistrustful, tend to lash out with words, toppling adversaries like tenpins. This is a worthy person whose nose for what's happening on the world scene and how to fix it is enviably accurate.

Sagittarius/Dog is a brash and opinionated sign. This person has an idea about everything and as his integrity is unquestionable, people tend to take what he or she says as gospel. Too, the Sagittarius/Dog is the opposite of cowardly. He or she dares much that others consider sheer madness. They speak out openly on all their ideas and they meet challenge with challenge. Ask a Sagittarius/Dog a question and he may toss you one right back. This character is a no-nonsense forger of ideals in his or her public life. They move in the best circles and make it their business to be seen in the "right" dinner parties and colloquiums. The Sagittarius/Dog is always taken seriously.

The nature here is generous. The soul is sensitivity itself. The Sagittarius/ Dog champions honor and sticks close to duty. He never shirks what he feels is the virtuous sector of life. However, as this person attaches so much importance to respectability, when he or she does let loose in private situations, the sky is the limit. This person indulges in pleasure as avidly as he or she plies a trade. Sagittarius/Dogs work at having a good time. And as they are thorough people, they leave no stone unturned in the debauchery department.

Sagittarius/Dog is a sign of leadership and fresh viewpoints. There is much creative thought in these people, and they will be able to apply that inventiveness to a career, since they are earth-connected and strict with themselves. These people know how to blend the Sagittarian's desire for expression and daring with the Dog's innate caution. They often become celebrated thinkers, writers, or linguists. They know how to align ideas and put them into words with flair and logic.

The Sagittarius/Dog is actually quite optimistic. The Dog's natural pessimism is jollied by Sagittarius's cheerfulness. Sagittarius also brings the Dog a certain cavalier attitude toward neatness and housekeeping. But never mind, the Dog returns the favor by making this Sagittarian more critical and less impetuous than normal. The marriage of Sagittarius to Dog gives us a powerful figure who sits comfortably on his or her throne.

If wronged, the Sagittarius/Dog will bite. This person does not take kindly to improbity. His methods are brash and his weapons king-sized. Never cross a Sagittarius/Dog unless you want to feel the sting of his slap for the rest of your born days. This person is basically peaceable, but approach him gently and don't try any funny business or he'll have your right leg. And if that doesn't make you understand, he'll take the left one too.

Love

In private situations these forceful people are remarkably sweet-natured. They sincerely want to be liked and despite a one-on-one shyness, they know how to involve themselves in a passionate way and can be faithful to that passion for a long time. They usually choose to keep their private affairs out of the public eye. They are masters of discretion in romantic matters. Sagittarius/Dogs never air their dirty linen for the world to see. They find "soap operatics" vulgar and dull.

Should you be smitten by this feisty character, you will not be able to keep him or her at home for long. The Sagittarius/Dog is always on the move. He or she takes on huge projects in public life and has stamina to burn for digging and turning over the earth to get to treasured goals. Your job will be to comfort and solace this nervous, sometimes disquieted soul. Your best bet is to have plenty to do on your own and not to wait up for your Sagittarius/

Dog lover to get home. They cannot recall when they rolled in before three A.M.

Compatibilities

You are a Tiger fan. Together you and the Tigers from Leo, Libra and Aquarius will go far. You also make beautiful music with Horse natives born in those same western astrological signs. Leo/Cats make you happy, too. They offer you optimism. You don't get much out of love affairs with Dragons, especially Gemini, Leo, Virgo and Pisces/Dragons. Gemini, Virgo and Pisces/Goats don't add anything to your life except anxiety, which you don't need. You just plain don't get on with Gemini/Monkeys.

Home and Family

The Sagittarius/Dog's family, its traditions and manners, its feast days and funerals, its ideals and coat of arms, will matter enormously to this person. However, in his own life, home is of practically no importance. He will want a nicely decorated flat or house near his office or place of work. But he doesn't want to fool around with putting up wallpaper or tiling the kitchen himself. This person is interested in his outside life and his work. If he can afford to, he will have maids and butlers to take care of housekeeping details.

Provided she can employ the best people to raise her children, this person will be a serious yet demanding parent. As respectability means a great deal to the Sagittarius/Dog, he will want kids to practice good manners and have gracious ways. As there is a bit too much crispness in the Sagittarius/Dog's emotional makeup, she must make a decided effort to be cuddly and warm with little ones. Also, if they are too conservative and strict with kids, these people can unwittingly form rebels who will return home at age twenty waving the banners of anarchy.

The Sagittarius/Dog child is a brittle little thing whose earnestness and desire to please and excel is touching. I would say this kid needs to be softened by nature and exposed to a little funk while still young in order to instill knowledge of how the other half lives. This child may be picky and nervous. Parents should encourage his or her writing talents and urge this child to achieve in areas where he can shine. No matter what you do, what interests the Sagittarius/Dog child is precisely what he or she will end up doing. They're like that—very directed, and independent as all get-out.

Profession

This character works very well in jobs that challenge his or her intellect. Sagittarius/Dogs have no time for pandering to obstreperous bosses or listening to office gossip. They go right to the desk and work till they drop. Then they leave their desks. They are abrupt and short-tempered in business dealings. Effectiveness is the single objective of this sharp-witted creature with the taste for freedom. He doesn't want to be tied to a job longer than he has to. She doesn't want to be restricted to her business except when necessary.

These people can make efficient bosses. They are, however, sarcastic and biting. Their manner is tough and no-nonsense, but their spirit is kindly. Understanding employees like them very much indeed. But weak people don't take well to the harsh environment engendered by this boss.

The Sagittarius/Dog will probably be serious in his work if employed, but he will surely be disobedient about trivial rules and flout them. Actually, the Sagittarius/Dog's dream is to work alone in some self-perpetuating pursuit or other like writing or running a hotel—or both.

Some suitable careers for Sagittarius/Dogs are: journalist, politician, novelist, linguist, translator, researcher, dramatist, activist, artist, lawyer, diplomat, speechwriter, professor.

Famous Sagittarius/Dogs: Jean Genet, Winston Churchill, Abe Burrows, Brooke Langton, David Kersh, Gianni Versace, Julie Condra, Louis Prima, Madchen Amick, Sophie Daumier, Steven Spielberg.

SAGITTARIUS

PIG

CHEERFULNESS	OUTSPOKENNESS	SCRUPULOUSNESS	CREDULITY
OPENHANDEDNESS	RECKLESSNESS	GALLANTRY	WRATH
SOLICITUDE	BAD MANNERS	SINCERITY	HESITATION
VALOR	VACILLATION	VOLUPTUOUSNESS	MATERIALISM
HONOR	CARELESSNESS	CULTURE	GOURMANDISM
REASON	CONTRADICTION	HONESTY	PIGHEADEDNESS

"I see"

Fire, Jupiter, Mutable

"I civilize"

Negative Water, Yin

Still waters run deep. The Sagittarian Pig, above reproach in moral conduct and beyond social disapprobation, makes it his or her business to maintain a spotless reputation. Don't think the Sagittarius/Pig is a Pollyanna and only capable of Boy Scoutism. Not at all. But this person attends to his or her public name by staying clear of trouble and acting the role of moralist.

Sagittarius/Pigs are born observers. They see everything that goes on around them and then some. They pick up on details and record speech patterns and tics. They recognize flaws and foibles in a wink and they find it all very amusing. When they are ready, armed with their closetful of human frailties, they synthesize their accumulated findings and send them back to us in the form of art. Sagittarius/Pig is a popular artist. Never too abstract or labyrinthine in his style, the Sagittarius/Pig's aim is to poke fun at society and, in turn, at himself.

These people have enormous public appeal. Nobody ever really feels threatened by a Sagittarius/Pig. The character is so constituted as to be unafraid of giving and caring openly about others. The Sagittarius/Pig is virtuous by nature and has an attractiveness that transcends physicality. In fact, I daresay, most Sagittarius/Pigs are not classically good-looking. But they have such honest, forthright charm that they can send entire populations swooning over their simple style.

They are sincerely interested in others. And what do people like better than talking about themselves? Sagittarius/Pig is an excellent listener who nods in all the right places and gives terrific, sound advice to people in trouble. Too, the Sagittarian Pig is indulgent with human failings. He or she truly can see why you argued with your baby sister on her wedding day. They are even touched by your weakness. How can anyone resist? Sagittarius/Pig is father and mother confessor in one and you don't have to recite any prayers as penance. I call Sagittarius/Pigs big-hearted.

But they can also be pigheaded. The Sagittarian born in a Pig year can get so caught up in his virtuousness that sometimes he forgets to be flexible. This causes plenty of trouble around the ranch. Of course the Sagittarius/Pig's sense of humor saves him from total rigidity. But his resistance to the ideas of others, or their suggestions, can be exasperating, to say the least.

Sagittarian Pigs are sometimes quixotic—and although their intentions are honorable, their attitudes can be brash or invasive. There is a tiny tendency here to engage in pratfall humor. I recommend intravenous subtlety. And attention. If the Sagittarius/Pig claims not to need applause, it's because he or she is ashamed to admit how much he thrives on it. Don't forget, Pigs are very cultivated people. The Pig born in Sagittarius must sometimes wonder who this rash and fiery beast he got into bed with at birth really is. Dauntless and even power-hungry, the Sagittarius/Pig runs a tight ship. But below decks there may be a party in full swing, the magnitude and exoticism of which would make Fellini faint from shock.

Love

Sagittarius/Pigs marry for love and often stay that way. These people are truly generous of spirit and giving of themselves. They are also utterly discreet and sincere. Of course the Sagittarius/Pig is interested in challenge from a lover or mistress, especially on an intellectual level. He will never be fully satisfied sharing a life with someone whose opinions he doesn't respect. Some great couples are half Sagittarius/Pig.

If you have fallen for one of these professional good guys, I know you must have a fine sense of humor. The Sagittarius/Pig is funny. He or she finds comedy everywhere. They are also gut-level appealing with their constant observations and their sense of humanity. Your position as the mate or companion of this finely tuned recording device will be to maintain your own autonomy and your reputation so that your Sagittarius/Pig can be proud of you. This person is not only interested in whether or not your tie is straight. The Sagittarius/Pig wants you to say clever things and know how to present your point of view. For Sagittarius/Pig, the image you present reflects directly on his sterling idea of self. To love you, the Sagittarius/Pig must believe in you too.

Compatibilities

You love the countryside. You cleave unto nature and sensuality, and extol the value of the hearth. Cats suit your need for household tranquility. Choose your own Cat from Aries, Leo, Libra or Aquarius. Leo and Aquarius/Goats are fine associates for you, too. Escape the clutches of Gemini, Virgo and Pisces/Snakes before they squeeze you to death. Gemini/Roosters are too scatty for your solid side, and Virgo/Monkeys too possessive.

Home and Family

The Sagittarian born in Pig years is such a busy person that his home will have to be first and foremost a functional place to work in. This is not the sort of person who comes home and takes off his shoes and flops onto a couch. He or she invariably goes straight from work to work. The desk may be plunk in the middle of the living room. This person loves precious things, but can dispense with opulence in favor of productivity.

Parenting interests the Sagittarian Pig because he's curious about human nature and fascinated by all its aspects. He will be generous with the time he spends with kids. She will read to them and listen sympathetically to their tales of school rivalries and difficult teachers. The Sagittarius/Pig is one of the most cuddly of the Sagittarian smoothies. Kids whose parents are born in this sign have a lot to live up to.

The Sagittarius/Pig child will show early signs of curiosity about the world. He will not be introverted or sulky. You can expect this child to work well in school and have fun with all things theatrical and creative. Too, his or her cynical comments will make you roar with laughter. These kids will survive almost all squabbles and family discord. They are uniquely self-propelled.

Profession

Reserve and will are the bywords of the Sagittarian Pig. He or she ought not to have very much trouble with career choices. They will be artistic for sure and able to turn their creative notions into viable vehicles for use in anything from business to entertainment or services. This person can be a winning performer or deft puppeteer. Whatever he or she does will be accompanied by good taste and a hearty dose of cheerfulness.

The Sagittarius/Pig is a fair and generous boss. He only demands perfection from people who work with and for him. But Pigs are honest and so are Sagittarians. Nobody can hate such a gallant soul.

The Sagittarian Pig employee is serious and reputable. You can trust him or her with the payroll. Of course, these people work splendidly alone. They undertake complex and difficult projects and over and over again make them successful.

Some careers suitable for the Sagittarius/Pig are: dramatist, film or theater director, actor, opera singer, composer, TV personality, lobbyist, clergyman, ecologist, cinematographer, photographer, inventor.

Famous Sagittarius/Pigs: Hector Berlioz, Phil Donahue, Woody Alien, Jules Dassin, Alain Bashung, Amy Locane, Chet Huntley, Christina Applegate, Claude Casadessus, Francis Huster, Freeman Dyson, Jane Birkin, Jean Pierre Foucault, Lee L. Cobb, Léon Schwartzenberg, Maria Callas, Michael McCary, Noël Coward, Nostradamus, Petra Kelly, Spike Jonz, Willy Brandt.

Other books by Suzanne White

CHINESE ASTROLOGY PLAIN AND SIMPLE

THE NEW ASTROLOGY

LA DOUBLE ASTROLOGIE

LA DOBLE ASTROLOGIA

THE NEW CHINESE ASTROLOGY

LA NEUVA ASTROLOGIA CHINA

THE ASTROLOGY OF LOVE

LADYFINGERS (A NOVEL)

BALD IN THE MERDE (A NOVELETTE)

Available in all formats (ebook and paper) from all Booksellers

Personal Telephone Readings, Books, Chapters, Horoscopes and Lifestyle
Advice at http://www.suzannewhite.com

12192808R00039

Printed in Germany
by Amazon Distribution
GmbH, Leipzig